Looking Back
ST. CLAIR SHIPPING
MARINE HIGHWAY

To my parents, Frank & Zine Mann
who realized and encouraged a love
of the St. Clair River

Looking Back

ST. CLAIR SHIPPING
MARINE HIGHWAY

Alan Mann

Looking Back Press

Copyright © 2006 by Alan Mann. All rights reserved. No part of this book may be reproduced, stored in a retrieval system, or transmitted in any form without written permission of the publisher.

Vanwell Publishing acknowledges the financial support of the Government of Canada through the Book Publishing Industry Development Program for our publishing activities.

Published by Looking Back Press
An Imprint of Vanwell Publishing Limited
1 Northrup Crescent, P.O. Box 2131
St. Catharines, ON L2R 7S2
For all general information contact Looking Back Press at:
Telephone 905-937-3100 ext. 829
Fax 905-937-1760
E-Mail vanessa.mclean@vanwell.com

For customer service and orders:
Toll-free 1-800-661-6136

Printed in Canada

National Library of Canada Cataloguing in Publication

Mann, Alan, 1936-
    St. Clair shipping: marine highway / Alan Mann.

(Looking back)
ISBN 1-55068-952-5

    1.Shipping-Saint Clair River (Mich. and Ont.)-History-Pictorial works. 2. Ships-Saint Clair River (Mich. and Ont.)-History-Pictorial works. 3. Saint Clair River (Mich. and Ont.)-History-Pictorial works. I. Title. II. Series: Looking back (St. Catharines, Ont.)

HE635.Z7S246 2006   386'.30971327   C2006-903994-1

Cover photo: The Belle River at Marine City, Michigan during winter layup 1904. (MHF)

A lady on deck of the *Tashmoo* with smoke in the background.

Contents

Acknowledgements	6
Introduction	7
Map	8
1. Wood and Steel: The Pioneers	9
2. Rivets and Steel: Metal Goliaths	19
3. Passenger Plans: Happy Decks	35
4. Brief Visitors: Short Stay Ships	53
5. Booms & Piles: Mountain Makers	63
6. War Route: Gray with Guns	71
7. Pleasure Plus: Speed with Class	77
8. U.S. Steel: Uncle Sam's Ships	91
9. Salties in St. Clair: Far from Home	101
10. Ferrying Frequently: Back and Forth	107
11. Preservation: Museum Quality	115
12. Canadian Content: Red Maple Leafs	121

Acknowledgements

With so many associates within my "marine circle" who also collect images, it was a simple matter of making requests for photo assistance. Sincere thanks are offered to the many who assisted: Bill Abraham, Ron Beauprè, Gene Buel, Bob Campbell, John Flick, Jim Gilbert, Skip Gillham, Esther Hankins, Blake Mann, Dan McCormack, Marguerite Myers, Gerry Ouderkirk, John Philbin, Jack Ridley. Special appreciations are extended to those who contributed a number of photos. Dick Wicklund with exceptional photographic skills offered a number of rare views. Ray Ingles, Lowell Dalgety and Bruce McMillan were helpful with the car ferry history. Al Jackson of Amherstburg came to the rescue by offering many exceptional images of salt water ships; many of the circumstances depicted Al, experienced himself through employment with McQueen Marine. George and David Lee, whose ancestors include local steamboaters back to the 1850s, offered many fine views of vessels, several owned or operated by their father Capt. Donald Lee. Sincere thanks to Bill Moran, whom I recall as an avid teenager showing encyclopedia-like potential for gathering and retaining facts about Great Lakes history. Within his contributions are images taken by Fr. Peter Vanderlinden, Paul Michaels, Dave Dennis. Thanks to them for recording Great Lakes history. Others have been helpful by providing specific information or through their encouragement. Thanks to Capt. Bill Hoey, Dr. Gordon Shaw, Gareth McNabb and many others who have been supportive in my efforts. A number of individuals no longer with us but most helpful in their day include Frank Crevier, Bill Luke, Alan Howard, Donald Lee, Capt. Donald Langridge, my father Frank Mann among others.

For the most part, images have been drawn from my own photo collection, first accumulated by my late father, who initially sparked my interest in the Great Lakes. Regretfully a number of images are unsourced, the photographers unknown but their efforts are appreciated. Some views are credited to the Detroit Marine Historical Society, my very first formal affiliate to study and preserve Great Lakes history. For pointing me towards the DMHS back in 1958, I thank the late Jack Miller who inspired and encouraged my interest. Many times he journeyed to Wallaceburg from his Michigan home so we could share photos while I was regaled by his many stories of ships and the Great Lakes.

At times, one's mind seems brimming with marine facts swimming around running into each other. To clear these muddles, the many reference sources available have been utilized. Availability of such centres of information is unlimited, such a contrast to when I started this passion several decades ago. Just a few books were available then, with little reference material stored. Locating a special ship on the St. Clair River occurred strictly by chance whereas now a vessel can be tracked wherever it is on the Great Lakes. The wonderful work of the many marine societies cannot be underestimated. Thanks to all those devoted individuals who follow marine history and report it seemingly as it happens. The newsletters from the various marine societies provide exceptional reference data.

Preservation of marine history, particularly of the St. Clair River area, has been well handled by the various museums on both sides of the international waterway. Thanks to the curators and volunteers who have provided data. It is hoped readers will be encouraged to explore these destinations. Thanks also to my family who withstand the inconveniences that accompany the pursuit of assembling a book. Thanks also to the very reliable Delina Bogaert for setting the text and Vanessa McLean and Looking Back Press for allowing me to share my passion with others.

Introduction

"I wish I could have!" The famed St. Clair River "flyer" *Tashmoo* ended her days the year I was born (1936). I wish I could have parked myself on the forward deck of the *Tashmoo* (like the pictured lady) and soaked up the stimulating St. Clair air, caught the occasional sniff of black smoke and endured the loud blasts of her steam whistle. And in this dream world, we may have passed the water slapping *Greater Detroit* or perhaps a much younger *John Ericsson*. In between the frequent ship sightings I would likely have scooted to a lower deck to gaze at items in the souvenir stand. Although I actually did see the vessels mentioned, the remainder of this scene is pure fantasy. Contentment must come now for "desired" marine experiences via photo images. Yet I am ever thankful I came along at a point in time when the St. Clair River was busy with many character vessels, be it the beat-up look of the old car ferry converted to the freighter *Carrolton* or the thumping diesel sounds of the Ford boats. And I was able to capture many of my river friends on film using a trusty Kodak box camera (620 film). And our summer cottage at Port Lambton (coming in 1942) was a bonus, placing me conveniently right at the river's edge.

Most of the vessels included herein are much like members of an extended family, their individuality recognized whether it be their deck configuration, whistle sound, paint scheme (I loved green hulls) or whether the hull had anchor pockets. These were some of the features I came to recognize and was often able to tell, from a distance, if my friend (such as the *James B. Eads*) was in view. I liked the *Eads* because of her flared bow and antiquity. The *Gleneagles* was like a queen to me, regal and important looking. And I thought it was nice of her to get stuck opposite our cottage in 1957, allowing a close-up view from our outboard. The *Lemoyne* was royal looking too, taking her time, and those early Imperial Oil tankers that seemed to be sinking caught my notice with their shrill whistles. One ship was my all-time favourite: *Stadacona (2)* in my estimation was a beautifully designed ship. Everything about her was just right. And a runner up would be *Oakglen (2)* raised a few notches when she donned her P & H paint scheme.

I did not sail myself but through (fortunate) circumstances enjoyed a number of adventures on water. The best was a 1960 five-day return trip from Detroit on a beautiful ship I had watched closely from the shoreline for years. What a thrill to be on the "white darling" *South America* looking in to shore, my perspective reversed as we waved to friends on that beautiful Sunday evening in August. A trip to Toronto on the former Georgian Bay passenger vessel *Normac* (guest of the Lee family) was another highlight, particularly locking through the Welland Canal. And an 11-day return trip from Sarnia aboard the Purvis tug *Wilfred M. Cohen* escorting the *Enerchem Refiner* to Sept-Iles, Quebec gave insight travelling on waters beyond Toronto. Seeing the colours of the Laurentians or the beluga whales frolicking in our wake are memories kept for a lifetime.

The collection of images within leans a bit on the lower St. Clair River area, my domain, with several early images of Wallaceburg and area ships. Although many were before my time I came to know them through stories of their adventures. They frequented the St. Clair River ports as well as penetrating the inland destinations, a chapter now a notation in history.

Many of the ships that ply the St. Clair River today seem somewhat impersonal and businesslike. They are included because they exuded character and are remembered for a reason such as the red Indian stack of the Wyandotte boats, the classy Misener line ships or even the names—Hutchinson, Shenago et al.

Enjoy this river journey as we go back … way back to the good old days!

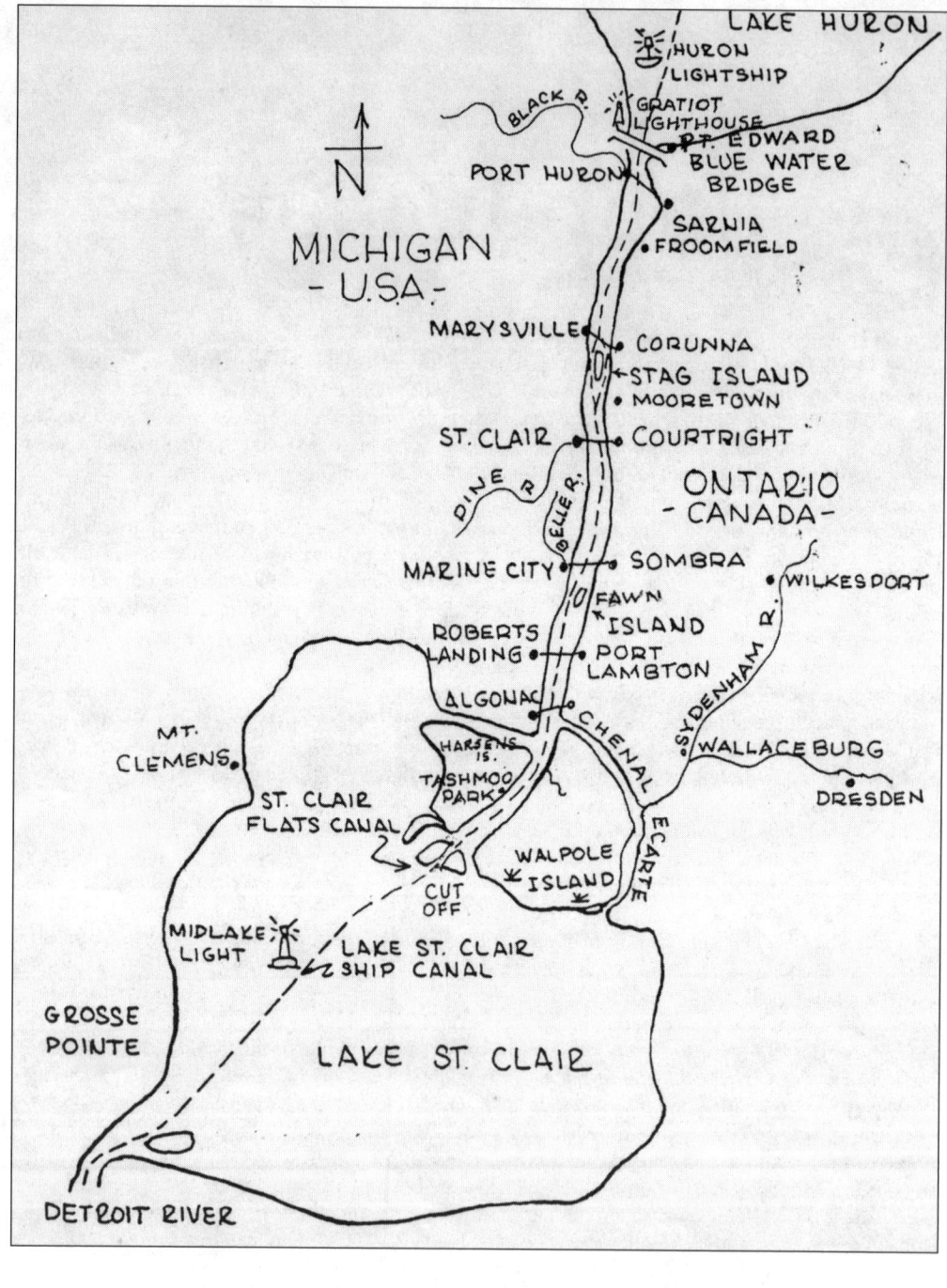

One
Wood & Steel
The Pioneers

Beacon from the north. The first welcome for ships to the St. Clair River is the historic Fort Gratiot Lighthouse which was constructed in 1829 by Lucas Lyon. Downbound mariners can detect the green flashing beacon from approximately 17 miles away, a welcome sight particularly during inclement weather. It was raised to its present 86 feet during the 1860s. Lighthouse keepers were on duty until 1933 when the light was automated. During 2006, Fort Gratiot Lighthouse became an historic site under the Port Huron Museum, joining the Huron Lightship (1990) and the 1944-built retired U.S. Coast Guard vessel *Bramble* (2003). (MHF)

Early river view. Two upbound steamers near Port Huron are about to head into Lake Huron in 1910. The riverscape is shown before the Blue Water Bridge was built, with its official opening not occurring until 25 May 1938. To the right on the Canadian shore is the Grand Trunk grain terminal at Point Edward. On the U.S. shoreline are vessels of the period including a schooner. Transporting rail cars across the busy waterway was begun in 1859 by the Grand Trunk Railroad. The first underground rail connection was in use by 1891 and a new tunnel was completed in 1995. (MHF)

One of the last. The schooner *Oliver H. Perry* was one of the last "wind" vessels on the Great Lakes. Built at Weymouth, Nova Scotia in 1919, the wooden vessel served on the Lakes as *J.T. Wing*. From 1939 to 1943 she was a familiar sight tied up at the McLouth Shipyard at Marine City, used mainly as a Sea Scout training vessel. In a valiant attempt at preserving schooner history, the vessel served briefly at Belle Isle as a museum ship, preceding eventual construction of the permanent Dossin Museum. On 2 November 1956 the grand old ship was purposely burned, as restoration and preservation would have been prohibitive. (MHF)

No sailing room. The *Lyman M. Davis* is moored at the Laird Lumber Co. wharf offloading cedar from the Georgian Bay woods. Her sails will not be unfurled while so far inland at the unlikely destination of Dresden, Ontario on the Sydenham River. Shown sometime during the 1890s, the schooner would travel under sail to the Chenal Ecarte at Walpole Island, be met by a steam tug that would tow the laden vessel through the tenuous 20-mile inland trip to Dresden, negotiating shallow water and twisting river turns along the way. (Ron Beaupre Collection)

Tight squeeze. The tug *W.H. Stone* and schooner *Burt Barnes* are in town with another load of lumber for the local building supplier in 1908 at Wallaceburg The vessels are paralleling the 1888-built bridge on the Sydenham River. The schooner was built at Manitowoc in 1882 and did most of her Canadian work after 1908 when she was purchased by the Graham Bros. of Kincardine, Ontario, engaged regularly thereafter in the St. Clair area. In 1924, nearing the end of her career the 95.5 foot vessel was bought by the James Swift Coal Co. of Kingston and was lost two years later on 1 September 1926 during a violent Lake Ontario storm. The tug *W.H. Stone* was built in 1889 at Sandusky, Ohio, spending much of her time escorting schooners inland to Dresden, Wilkesport and Wallaceburg. (MHF)

Tunnel on the move. This dramatic view taken by Louis Pesha in 1909 shows the tug *C.B. Lowan*, downbound off Walpole Island, and a prefabricated section of the Michigan Central Rail Tunnel being constructed under the Detroit River. The huge components were constructed at the Great Lakes Engineering Co. yard at St. Clair, Michigan with the wooden framework used to encase concrete. An amazing engineering feat, the busy tunnel continues to serve rail interests linking Canada and the United States. (Pesha photo from MHF)

Layup time. The Belle River at Marine City has enjoyed a rich and busy history particularly during the era when hundred of vessels were built at this busy St. Clair River port. During winter layup, the narrow river was jammed with vessels, some seemingly shoehorned into position for a winter rest. Lumber hookers, tugs, schooners, barges were all there indicating a rich marine heritage in the community where many officers and crew made their homes. Opposite the *D.F Rose* is the schooner *Thomas Down*, moored at the Sicken Lumber Co. dock. The views circa 1904, offer a wide contrast to today when only pleasure craft frequent the once commercially clogged waterway. (MHF)

Belles of the river. The ice has cleared, the Belle River is flowing and crews are awaiting the spring call. In Marine City, a sailors' town, there will soon be regular exchanges of waves from shore to ship as the many vessels pictured have completed their winter sojourn. This 1904 scene showing winter layup at Marine City is a good indicator of how important commercial shipping was to the community. A number of the vessels shown are home for winter as they were built in the various shipyards nearby. (MHF)

Langell boys. Langell was a most familiar family name around the Marine City area, and this attractive vessel moored near the Belle River carried the prominent designation to many points around the Great Lakes. The 387 ton, 151 foot vessel was built upriver at St. Clair in 1890, but would be seen regularly around Marine City. The vessel was noted for her most attractive exterior paint scheme, a pleasant effect shown after the ship was lengthened at the McLouth Shipyard in Marine City during 1921. Ten years later, 13 June 1931, the vessel sank in Lake Huron. (MHF)

W.S. Ireland. When lumber was king in the St. Clair area during the 19th century, the economy on both sides of the river was booming. Felling the stands of timber and turning it into building lumber, barrel staves, firewood and other products created a strong base for the various communities along the river strip. To transport these products, small steam powered vessels such as the pictured 86 foot *W.S. Ireland* were plentiful in the area. This vessel was built at the McDonnell Shipyard in Wallaceburg in 1872. The upper deck shows the galley chief ready to ring the dinner bell while captain and crew stand by. The *W.S. Ireland's* tonnage dues payable to the Dominion government in 1876 are noted as $12.28 which includes a $5.00 inspection fee. Although seeming rather miniscule in comparison to today's cost, this amount was likely a solid hit to the vessel's profit figure. (MHF)

Highbanks twin. The popularity of excursion boats during the last half of the 19th century is exemplified by the two pictured day boats moored at Highbanks Park, on Walpole Island near the mouth of the Chenal Ecarte. *The City of Chatham* and the *Trerice*, both popular for bringing inland residents of Kent County to the open waters of Lake St. Clair and the St. Clair River, are shown during the 1890s. Other locales on their route included Stag Island, also Belle Isle. During the return trips, the journey of several hours saw passengers much more subdued, many yawning or asleep after soaking up the refreshing "excursion boat air." (MHF)

Cold storage. William Colwell, a local department store owner, oversees this bitter winter scene at Wallaceburg in 1919. With lots of ice on the Sydenham River, layup near the local shipyard shows a large unit from the Chatham Dredge Co., the hull remains of the *American Eagle* and the tug *Harry Sewell*. Once spring arrives and fitting out is underway again, the many ports in the St. Clair area spring back to life. (MHF)

Side launch. The Sidney McLouth Shipyard at Marine City turned out numerous wooden vessels during the busy shipbuilding era. It is an historic site still in operation as an aggregates supplier. Shown is one of its many ship launches, this one the *Oliver H. Perry*, splashing into the St. Clair River in 1921. The 87 foot vessel was built for the Ohio Fisheries Commission serving until 1938 when it was reconstructed for work in northern Michigan and became the *Mackinac Islander*. In 1968 the venerable vessel went to the west coast. Regrettably she sank with all hands in 1974 near the Aleutian Islands. (MHF)

Wm. F. McRae. All hands are on deck for the photographer's lens. This busy tug which worked hauling barges inland and in the St. Clair River district, was built at the McDonnell Shipyard in Wallaceburg in 1880. At 65 feet the tug could penetrate easily through inland waters to pick up shallow draught barges laden with lumber, staves or firewood. In 1895 the tug ran into difficulty and sank in Lake Huron. However her time was not over as the hull was raised, repaired and put back into service. The *McRae* was dismantled at Sorel, Quebec in 1923 after a busy 43 years of service. (MHF)

D.A. Gordon (1). This 1902 view shows activity at the Lee Shipyard at Wallaceburg with the 115 foot wooden ship *D.A. Gordon* taking shape. With master shipbuilder Jack Scagel in charge, the vessel was side launched and put into service mainly in the St.Clair River area. In 1905 the vessel was rebuilt, adding extra cargo space as owner John Lee extended his customer load. The *D.A. Gordon* had a relatively short working career as fire consumed the hull in 1909 at Port Arthur, Ontario. A few years later another vessel with the same name would be built in Scotland, both honouring David Alexander Gordon, an influential industrialist in Wallaceburg. (MHF)

John Lee. James Paris Lee is credited with perfecting the world famous Lee Enfield repeating rifle in Wallaceburg. His brother John Lee enjoyed an interest in weapons but made his name in shipping. His namesake vessel, built in 1888 at Wallaceburg, is shown moored at the company dock. Utilized in both freight and passenger trade, the vessel was rebuilt in 1890, with components from the tug *A.T. Kelly* and a boiler from the *Interoceon*. In April of 1900 Lee Steamship Co. sold the vessel to the Collingwood Steamship Co. for use in the upper lakes until 8 August 1913 when fire took the historic hull at Port McNicholl, Ontario. (MHF)

Four abreast. Capt. James Davidson of Bay City, Michigan, was the brains and money behind the building of a massive sugar processing plant in Dresden during 1902. Given a municipal bonus of $40,000, the inland community on the Sydenham River was elated at the economic boom. However, just as the plant was in operation the following year an assessment disagreement prompted Davidson to abruptly end operations. Calling Dresden council's bluff, the resolute Davidson dismantled the plant and loaded components onto two of his schooners, *Paisley* and *Grampian* (shown at Wallaceburg) and moved everything to Janesville, Wisconsin, in one of the most surprising events ever recorded in Western Ontario. (MHF)

Swing it Rose! Launch day in shipbuilding communities was a special occasion, the townsfolk attending in full force. On this day, 23 May 1924, the namesake of the vessel, Miss Rose Burgess, is about to swing the ceremonial bottle of champagne against the new steam barge *Rose Burgess*, launched at the McDonnell Shipyard in Wallaceburg. School children were given a half holiday to witness the launching. The 423 ton vessel served mainly in the St. Clair River area with the occasional venture into Lake Erie. She finished her career in the St. Lawrence River during the 1940s. (MHF)

Two
Rivers & Steel
Metal Goliaths

Howard and seven wading ladies. On a hot summer day in the late 1930s the pictured ladies could not resist cooling down in the St. Clair River at Port Lambton. Content with the cooling, they are likely oblivious to the wake that will soon be sent ashore by the upbound *Howard M. Hanna* passing routinely; light and fast, unaware of the screams and shrieks she is about to cause. No need for great alarm however as the further dunking will likely be refreshing. (Esther Hankins Collection)

D.A. GORDON (2). While the first vessel under this name was a wooden vessel, the hull pictured here at Wallaceburg was steel, built in 1910 at Glasgow, Scotland. This 249 foot ship was built for the Canadian Shipbuilding Co. under the partnership of David A. Gordon and Henry Munderloh. The *D.A. Gordon* was the first of several ships planned to carry products of the Canada & Dominion Sugar Co., which operated plants across Canada. However the *D.A. Gordon* was the only one built as war intervened and the ship was requisitioned for convoy duty. On 11 December 1917 the *D.A. Gordon* was sunk by enemy action off the coast of Spain. The vessel is shown at the Wallaceburg plant in 1911. (MHF)

Sarnia City. This 105 foot steel tug built in 1893 at Toledo as *Detroiter* became familiar in the Sarnia area with Reid Shipwrecking Co. The tug was rebuilt at Sarnia in 1910 and worked the St. Clair area for years. In 1928 she was sold to Sincennes-McNaughton. In 1941 the tug was sent to the east coast during the Second World War and was eventually dismantled. (MHF)

James B. Eads. Billows of black smoke and a sharply flared bow were the familiar signs of this Great Lakes veteran. Built by Globe Iron Works at Cleveland in 1894 (named *Globe*) the 417 foot classic steamer joined Upper Lakes Shipping in 1935. She put in 68 faithful years of service before being dismantled in 1967 at Port Weller, Ontario. During her working career she provided excellent service for owners and much satisfaction to those who appreciated classic lines. *James B. Eads* called at Sarnia elevators on many occasions, usually drawing special attention from ship lovers. (Fr. Vanderlinden, Moran Collection)

Sulphite. This tall stack tug with beautiful classic lines was built far from the Great Lakes, in 1919 at Elizabeth, New Jersey as *Ballew*. She came to fresh water in 1924 towing pulp barges from upper lakes ports to Detroit, thus being a familiar sight in the St. Clair River. In 1956, Hindman Transportation of Owen Sound was her final owner but this company used the tug infrequently. Dismantling came in Goderich in 1966, a regretful end to such a handsome vessel. (MHF)

Frosted Maple(ton). A late season departure from Wallaceburg on 4 December 1940 shows the C.S.L. package freighter breaking ice in the Sydenham River after taking on a load of refined sugar and glassware. The *Mapleton* worked in support of the war effort as did other "tiny" ships of her style, some even venturing overseas as part of convoys. Built in 1909 in England, this 250 foot canaller was sold to foreign interests in 1948 and was reportedly burned in the Suez area in 1950, far from the Great Lakes. (MHF)

Clary Forhan. Moored at the Canada & Dominion Sugar Co. wharf in Wallaceburg during the summer of 1950, this Sarnia Steamship bulker was built in Scotland in 1929 as *Côteaudoc* for Paterson Steamship. The 259 foot vessel was back in the Atlantic during the Second World War and survived convoy duty. Renamed *Milverton* in 1946, *Clary Forhan* in 1949, the vessel was finally scrapped in 1963 under the name *Ferndale*. On this particular trip *Clary Forhan* brought in raw sugar and took away the refined variety, the latter loaded by hand carts. (MHF)

City of Toronto. The signature ship of the Toronto Marine Historical Society, this handsome canaller was a familiar visitor to both Sarnia and Wallaceburg, taking on mixed cargo. Pictured at the government wharf in Wallaceburg 3 July 1941, the vessel is about to dock where glass, brass and agricultural products will be loaded. The *City of Toronto* was built in 1926 at Davie Shipbuilding, Lauzon, Quebec and was bustling about the Great Lakes until the St. Lawrence Seaway opening put the now small and obsolete canallers out of work. Scrapping came in 1961 at the same yard where she was built. (MHF)

Hagarty. Upbound near Cherry Beach (south of Marine City) in 1958, the 550 ft. bulker was a Collingwood product, launched 18 June, 1914 as *J.H.G. Hagarty* for the Chicago and St. Lawrence Steam Navigation Co. Her name was shortened to *Hagarty* in 1926. The vessel was acquired by Canada Steamship Lines in 1917, sailing faithfully until her retirement in 1967. The attractive coal burner was a frequent visitor to the St. Clair River area, usually hauling grain from the upper lakes. As was the fate of many Great Lakes favourites, she was scrapped overseas in Spain during 1968, a sad end to a proud ship. (Bill Abraham Photo)

Lovely Lady. The cement carrier *S.T. Crapo* was early to sail and late to layup for many seasons of her career. Running between Alpena and Detroit or Cleveland, this "traditional" looking vessel was a familiar sight on the St. Clair River, often the first ship of the season. The 1927-built bulker often bucked ice, but on this voyage, 5 September 1995, it was a beautiful, calm late summer day in the St. Clair River near Robert's Landing. With a sky behind her and barely rippling waters in her path the downbound passage was a sight for the memory books. At the invitation of the photographer she even gave a friendly salute, the steam shooting from a vintage steam whistle, another indication of her classic status. Time eventually became an enemy as the *S.T. Crapo* last operated on her own on 4 September 1996, exactly one year after her image was captured for perpetuity. She survives as a storage hull for Inland Lakes Management Inc., being shuttled around to various locations. The vessel will be best remembered however when smoke emitted from her stack and flows of beautiful steam shot from her whistle. (MHF)

Busted Nose? An untimely career end came for this Canada Steamship Lines mid size package freighter on 1 June 1967. After *Renvoyle* departed the C.S.L. freight sheds dock at Point Edward, the menacing St. Clair rapids caught the 390 ft. vessel, swung her to the U.S. side where she rammed the moored *Sylvania,* unloading at the Peerless Cement dock. The *Sylvania* sank and the *Renvoyle* slunk away with a badly bent bow. Repairs proved too costly for the C.S.L. ship and she was scrapped at Ashtabula. *Sylvania* was repaired and returned to service for her owners, Tomlinson Line. (MHF)

Lemoyne and Loved. To Canada Steamship Line the 620 ft. *Lemoyne* was the pride of their fleet. For ship lovers, her handsome styling with the "fat stack," layers of cabins and classic lines cultivated a wide following. The "C.S.L. Queen" participated in opening ceremonies for the fourth Welland Canal in August of 1932. This grand lady served faithfully until retired in 1968. The vessel enjoyed many firsts over a remarkable career, giving the ship a reputation that endured for many years. *Lemoyne* slipped away in 1969, a sad ending thrust upon the fine old ship when towed overseas for scrapping in Spain. (MHF)

Last Two Out. Here the 1959 season is underway (despite ice still moving in the St. Clair River) and a previously packed Sarnia harbour is down to its last two winter residents. The venerable Upper Lakes bulker *Howard L. Shaw* has steam up and is nearly ready to go, while her neighbour *R. Bruce Angus* will not be far behind in joining the spring parade. The *"Angus"* came out in 1951 as *Imperial Redwater*. The elder *"Shaw"* had operated for 59 years by the time this view was photographed. She retired in 1967 but her hull remains as an Ontario Place breakwall at Toronto. The original oil tanker *"Angus"* was converted to dry cargo for Upper Lakes in 1952-53 and lasted until 1985 when sold for scrap. (MHF)

Sarnia Squeeze. A haven for winter ship watchers, Sarnia harbour is jammed for a 1940s layup. The Upper Lakes veteran *Douglass Houghton* leads the pack with a total of eight vessels marshalled into line. Come spring, an orderly departure is necessary before each hull hits open water. A short distance away is another winter layup spot, the North Slip, located in Point Edward. (MHF)

Steelvendor. Moored inland at Wallaceburg in July of 1923, this 225 ft. vessel is unloading 1800 tons of raw sugar beets at the nearby Canada & Dominion Sugar Co. plant. This was a rather unusual cargo for the relatively new ship since she was designed to carry steel products (reason for her name). However, during the 1920s, companies would contract for any type of cargo to keep their ships operating. *Steelvendor* called at this port only this one year. In 1942 she plunged to the bottom in a mishap on Lake Michigan. (MHF)

Paterson A+ Smoke. Perhaps fashionable at the time but not environmentally friendly, the Paterson canaller *Newbrundoc* (built in England,1928) puts up a great smoke screen on the St. Clair River opposite Walpole Island. The 260 ft. vessel handled a variety of bulk cargoes and was a frequent visitor to the St. Clair River area, stopping at Sarnia and Wallaceburg. Her final season came in 1963 and like many canallers that were pushed aside by larger vessels, *Newbrundoc* was scrapped that year. Time is May of 1962, her second last season. (MHF)

Pig or Cigar? A special attraction during her final years, mainly because she was one of the last of her breed, the *John Ericsson* is shown on the St. Clair River heading to Sarnia where she loaded frequently. The unique rounded hull was called by some a pig boat, others used the term cigar boat. The 390 ft. vessel came out in 1896, a product of the American Steel Barge Co., Superior, Wisconsin. By 1938 the whaleback was with Upper Lakes & St. Lawrence Co. working faithfully for the Canadian company until retirement in 1963. The *John Ericsson* was scrapped five years later, following an attempt to preserve this unique ship as a museum. (George Lee Collection)

Pointe Noire. This traditional looking bulker, spouting steam, is shown moored at the Sarnia elevators on 3 November 1979 taking on grain. The vessel came out as the *Samuel Mather (4)* for Interlake Steamship in 1926. Transfer to Canadian flag for Upper Lakes came in 1968. The 581 ft. bulker put in 12 more years until laying up 12 December, 1980 at Toronto. A frequent visitor to the St. Clair River with many stops at Sarnia, *Pointe Noire* was scrapped at Port Maitland during 1982-1983. (MHF)

Glasstown. Opening navigation in a port reaps traditional rewards…usually a ceremonial top hat. When Capt. L.H. Young brought the Upper Lakes steamer *James Stewart* to Wallaceburg 6 April 1975, he was surprised when presented with a set of tumblers produced locally at the Dominion Glass Co. Dressed formally for the presentation, Capt. Young is shown with Chamber of Commerce officials Louis Puskas and Jock Appleton. The *Stewart* hauled away 100,000 bushels of soya beans on this occasion. (MHF)

Goodbye Henry. Nearing the end of a busy career this 9 July1987 view of the Kinsman's *Henry Steinbrenner (4)* is opposite the mouth of the Chenal Ecarte River south of Port Lambton. Built in 1916 as *William A. McGonagle* at Cleveland, the 580 ft. bulker was taken over by Kinsman in 1984. Layup came in 1989 and scrapping at Port Maitland in 1994, the second last coal burning carrier on the Great Lakes. A frequent visitor to the St. Clair River area, the vessel's classic lines were especiallly admired during her final sailing years. (MHF)

Nicolet. An American steamship self-unloader that gained a few extra years late in her career is shown 3 August 1989 upbound at Port Lambton. Sporting a new pilot house, the 533 ft. vessel last operated 20 December 1990, laying up at Toledo. Built in 1905 she came out as *William G. Mather*. A frequent visitor to the St. Clair River serving a remarkable 85 years, *Nicolet* became a favourite. Finally scrapped during 1996-1997 when towed to Port Maitland by the tug *Otis Wack*. (MHF)

George M. Carl. While the *Texaco Brave* (left) stands guard, the 1922-built bulker *George M. Carl*, a Misener ship, takes on grain at the Sarnia elevator in 1973. The 617 ft. bulker came out in 1922 as *Fred G. Hartwell* for Franklin Steamship, sailing under that name until 1954 when renamed *Matthew Andrews* for Hanna Coal & Ore Corp. On 29 November 1962 the vessel was acquired by Scott Misener Steamship Co. and given her pictured name. A frequent visitor to Sarnia, the attractive vessel finished an active career in 1982 and was scrapped in Spain two years later. (MHF)

H.C. Heimbecker. Most attractive in her senior years when given a fancy paint scheme by Soo River Company, this long serving laker became a special ship to many. Built in 1905 for Pittsburgh Steamship, her classic lines, traditional steam whistle, and her antiquity gave the vessel special notice. First named *George W. Perkins* when built at Superior for Pittsburgh Steel, she sailed until laid up in 1960. New life came when bought by Westdale Shipping and renamed in 1964 as *Westdale (2)*. In 1977 the 569 ft. bulker still had life and sailed for Robert Pierson Holdings, later Soo River Co. A stretched career came to an end in 1981 due to a cracked boiler forcing retirement and dismantling later that year. But *H.C. Heimbecker* made a lasting impression. (Bob Campbell Photo)

Oakglen (1). Pictured on the St. Clair River near Algonac during the summer of 1988, this P & H Shipping vessel is downbound near the end of a busy career. Built in Lorain as *William H. Warner* the 580 ft. bulker would take on three more names, *International* in 1934, *Maxine* in 1977 and *J.F. Vaughn* in 1981. The vessel was registered Canadian 15 April 1982 when taken over by Pierson Holdings. Sailing for Soo River, the end came in May of 1988 when the 1923-built vessel was sold for scrap but sailed under her own power down the lakes, headed for Sorel for an overseas tow to Turkey. *Oakglen* is shown during her final trip in the St. Clair River. Chief engineer Ralph Morris of Goderich has already dismantled the ship's steam whistle which was kept for posterity. (MHF)

Cambria. Somewhat unique with her interesting deck apparatus, and classed as a crane ship, the 1910-built vessel was originally a strait decker named *E.U. Utley*. In 1924 the 504 ft. ship was purchased by Bethlehem Transportation, was converted to the pictured guise in 1955, and served that company until 1970. Ownership changes saw the ship passed around, but always attracting extra attention from ship fans particularly in the St. Clair River area. Her end came in 1973. (Fr. Vanderlinden, Moran Collection)

Ben E. Tate. Versatile and reliable, at ease in either open or confined waters, this strait decker turned self unloader was familiar in the St. Clair River for many years. Built in 1902 as *Panay* the 376 ft. ship became *William Nelson* in 1928 before taking on her final name, *Ben E. Tate*, in 1936. Serving faithfully and generally accident free, the *"Tate"* made money for her various owners over a six decade career. Like many other "friends of the St. Clair" she ended up on a towline overseas, being scrapped in Spain during 1969. (MHF)

Chicago Tribune. This one-of-a-kind ship, built in 1930 at Hull, England, worked mainly as a pulp wood carrier. The ship was easily identified by the unique extension vertically of her deck. First named *Thorold*, the 258 ft. canaller took on the name of a well known Chicago newspaper in 1933. During her final years the vessel was mastered by the popular Capt. John Leonard, a legend himself who regaled others with his ship stories. In 1988 the vessel was sold for scrap and was dismantled at Port Colborne, her loss a sad one for the shipping scene. (Fr. Vanderlinden, Moran Collection)

Amoco Michigan. The St. Clair River was graced whenever the *Amoco* tankers sailed by. Some loved the sound of their steam whistles, others adored their tall stacks. The *Amoco Michigan* was first to go from the American Oil fleet. Built by American Shipbuilding Co. at Lorain in 1927 as *Robert W. Stewart*, the 379 ft. tanker was retired in 1967. She was sold overseas in 1969 and finished her days as a bunkering barge. (Fr. Vanderlinden, Moran Collection)

Harry Coulby. A touch of class came with the *Coulby* wherever she went. The beamy bow pushing phosphorescent water put her in the queen class. A 1927 product from Lorain's American Shipbuilding Co., and always a straight decker, the *Coulby* plodded along until 1981 when the 631 ft. ship was laid up by Interlake. A reprieve came in 1989, returning to service for Kinsman, renamed *Kinsman Enterprise,* sailing a second life until December of 1995. During 2005-2006 the retired ship was scrapped at Port Colborne. (Fr. Vanderlinden, Moran Collection)

Imperial Windsor. Launched as *Windsolite* on 5 April 1927 in England, this frequent Sarnia visitor had the distinction of being the last canal-sized tanker to serve in the Imperial Oil fleet. In 1947 in keeping with a new naming system, the 256 ft. vessel was renamed *Imperial Windsor*. She spent most of her time running between Sarnia and Montreal but did work on the east coast. After being busy the first two years of the 1970s she was idled at Sarnia in 1972 and in 1973 became *Cardinal* of Algonquin Shipping. After a collision with *Henry Steinbrenner* on 23 May 1974 she was scrapped later that year. (Dave Dennis, Moran Collection)

Three
Passenger Plans
Happy Days

City Of Toledo. The White Star dock at Port Lambton was busy as the only Canadian dockage (other than Sarnia) for the daily runs from Detroit to Port Huron until 1936, when excursion service ended. Shown is the (one-stack) *City of Toledo* heading downbound from Port Lambton in 1914 after disembarking a few hundred excursionists who enjoyed a few hours on the St. Clair River. Built in Toledo in 1891, the vessel was acquired by White Star in 1895 for the day run north from Detroit. (MHF)

Upper Deck Rendezvous. Day trips arranged by lodges, service clubs and church groups proved popular during a period when few owned automobiles and an excursion trip was reasonably priced. The *Omar D. Congar, Ossifrage, Rapids King, Thousand Islander, Owana, Pelee* are but notations in history. Yet in their day the cool, refreshing waters of the St. Clair area, combined with a tasty picnic lunch attracted excursionists, particularly from inland points such as Dresden, Wallaceburg and Chatham. As added enjoyment, the ship's orchestra often provided the perfect musical touch. Here excursionists from Wallaceburg, shown aboard the *Omar D. Congar* in 1914, are dressed in their finest. The young lads with skimmers are either readying for a deck game of blind man's bluff or perhaps keeping cool on a hot (upper deck) summer day on the St. Clair River. (MHF)

Wee Winona. Small, but all the better for negotiating the twists and turns of the narrow shoals of inland waters, the passenger steamer *Winona* was stationed in Wallaceburg from 1904 to 1906. Regularly scheduled trips for the Detroit-Wallaceburg Steamship Co. carried hundreds of happy excursionists to nearby points such as Stag Island, Sarnia and occasionally across the lake to Belle Isle. Capt. Walter Power knew the narrow Sydenham and Chenal Ecarte rivers like the back of his hand, with a miss on the mud solved by simply putting engines astern. A return trip from Wallaceburg to the St. Clair and back was advertised at 35 cents. (MHF)

Pelee. Built primarily for the cross Lake Erie run, the newly built steamer *Pelee* instead spent the 1914 season (her first) running a day excursion service between Detroit and Wallaceburg. Built at Collingwood in 1914 at 137 ft. for the Windsor & Pelee Island Steamship Co., the first season running excursions was a good test for the ship that would battle choppy seas on Lake Erie for the next several years. Shown at Wallaceburg as a brand new ship for a day trip to the St. Clair River, the vessel ran the cross Erie service until 1960 and languished thereafter at Port Stanley until finally demolished in 1973, her last few years unhappy ones. (MHF)

Omar D. Congar. This popular steamer was built in 1882 at Port Huron, home for her entire career. However, Wallaceburg was a second home as service from that port started in 1904 and continued until 1921, the last year of service for the pert excursion vessel. She was also used for ferry service between Port Huron and Sarnia but day excursions became her specialty. An afternoon cruise from Wallaceburg in 1919 was just 40 cents while the moonlight cruise was 60 cents. Regretfully the *Omar D. Congar* was destroyed while fitting out for the new season 26 March 1922 when an overheated boiler exploded. (MHF)

Rapids King. Another popular day steamer that added to the St. Clair River ship parade was the Northern Navigation vessel *Rapids King*. And "rapid" she was, as evidenced by this speeding vessel heading to Wallaceburg in 1923 shearing a path on the mirror-like Chenal Ecarte River. Although the route was not profitable for Northern Navigation, little did financial affairs bother happy patrons. (MHF)

Thousand Islander. During the 1920s this Northern Navigation day steamer beat a regular path from Detroit to Chatham, or Wallaceburg on alternate days. A full trip fare in 1921 was $1.50 with a Saturday night moonlight special also available. It was a laid-back world with a few cents, picnic basket and sense of adventure the only ingredients for a time well spent. The famed Baldoon Mystery, a Chenal Ecarte attraction, was popularized by the excursion vessels as a means of adding some intrigue to the several hours' return trip. An hour off the ship for shopping was another feature of the day trip. (MHF)

Ossifrage. It is 1918, the war is nearly over and the sleek day boat *Ossifrage* is ready to depart with a full load of passengers from Wallaceburg, heading to Belle Isle. The ship's orchestra will be playing joyful tunes, the souvenir stand will be busy and an air of happiness will pervade the decks of the ship. The return voyage will be much more relaxed as a pleasant and memorable day brings on yawns and short naps, another experience to remember during the days when excursion vessels plied the marine highways. (MHF)

City Of Chatham. Another popular inland favourite frequenting Chatham and Wallaceburg, the vessel, built by Polson Iron Works in 1888 in Toronto, sailed that route along with Detroit as a destination until 1909. At 136 ft. the day steamer was well suited for the narrow inland routes bringing much joy and relaxation to the many who frequented her decks over the years. The vessel was sold to the St. Joe's Island and Soo Line and ran in the northern area until 1921 but was fondly remembered for her many years in southwestern Ontario. The vessel is shown on the Sydenham River heading for open waters in 1906. (MHF)

Tashmoo Park. Centrepiece of the White Star Line's Detroit to Port Huron excursion run during the first few decades of the 20th century, Tashmoo Park was located at Sans Souci on Harsen's Island. Opened in 1896 and acquired by White Star Line in 1899, the 60 acre site with its casino and unique cupolas expanded by the 1920s with mechanical entertainment. *Tashmoo* the steamer is shown at Tashmoo Park dock where hundreds would be dropped off daily, picked up a few hours later after the boat returned from the Port Huron run. Interest dropped off when families had their own automobiles and the once famous Tashmoo Park closed in 1951. (MHF)

Tashmoo Remnant. After a grounding in 1936 in the Detroit River, subsequent pumping operations which were carried out incorrectly broke the back of the popular steamer *Tashmoo*. Capt. James McKenty of Chatham was successful in acquiring the entire pilothouse at an auction. The section was shipped to Mirwin's Park, a recreational centre west of Wallaceburg on the Chenal Ecarte River. McKenty turned the structure into a summer home. But *Tashmoo's* popularity continued, with many admiring or asking for a tour. On June 10,1951 a fire destroyed the final large remainder of the White Star Line's famous vessel *Tashmoo*, still immortal to many. (MHF)

North West. The pictured scene at Stag Island shows the original beauty of this white-hulled steamer. The *North West* was built in 1894 by the Globe Iron Works in Cleveland for the Great Northern Railway Co. as a passenger vessel. An identical ship called *North Land* was built a year later. They were routed between Duluth and Buffalo. Quite palatial, white-hulled with three stacks they were glorious looking vessels with a star on the centre funnel. They were built to compete with the Detroit & Cleveland Navigation Co. ships but unfortunately became two white elephants for their owners, their 28 boilers being very costly to operate. The elegant but expensive to run *North West* (at 385 ft.) was damaged by fire during Buffalo layup in 1911. After the fire the vessel languished for a few years until 1918 when there was a shortage of steel hulls for wartime needs. The hull was cut in two and while in transit for rebuilding, the bow section broke away and sank during a storm in November of 1918. The after end was taken to Montreal and a new bow section was added at Lauzon, Quebec. In 1920 the vessel took on an entirely new role, rebuilt with one less stack and more efficient engines as a wrecking vessel. Sold to Canada Steamship Lines in 1921, the renamed *Maplecourt* again returned to Lakes service and was often stationed in Sarnia. The vessel was cut in two once more in 1922. The intact ship was caught in a severe Lake Huron storm 20 October 1929 and spent the winter lodged on a rocky reef. Salvaged by Sin-Mac Lines the vessel was repaired and put to work as a salvage vessel, then sold to United Towing & Salvage in 1937 and seen regularly in the Sarnia area. During the Second World War the ship was requisitioned by the Canadian government and cut in two for the third time at Kingston and rejoined at Montreal. Engaged in convoy duty carrying vital supplies overseas, *Maplecourt* departed from Sydney 22 January 1941, but fell victim to a U-boat attack by *U 107* and was sunk with all hands on 7 March, 1941. (Jim Gilbert Collection)

Roosevelt Up. Sisters Sue and Midge Woodward sit ashore while their daddy Bill is pulling up pike and perch for supper. Beyond, the *Theodore Roosevelt* is hosting another load of excursionists enjoying their journey on the scenic St. Clair River, soon passing the international community cousins of Roberts Landing, Michigan and Port Lambton, Ontario in this peaceful 1938 scene, one year before the outbreak of the Second World War. (Esther Hankins Collection)

Finale. It is 1949, an early Friday morning in July at Port Lambton when the box camera of a 13-year-old (the writer) captured this image of the *Greater Detroit* downbound at Port Lambton. Little was it realized at the time that the end for the historic *D & C* fleet was looming, 1949 being their final season of operation. The camera memory captures that eventful day. (MHF)

Hamonic Harmony. At the Sarnia waterfront during the Second World War the harbour was busy with freighters, ships of many descriptions were passing up and down the waterfront and a wartime ship building program was underway at Mac-Craft Industries. The pictured 1942 scene shows in the foreground a newly built Fairmile, *QO 63* being fitted out prior to departure for war service. Another impending departure shows the Northern Navigation steamer *Hamonic* ready to pull out after a winter layup in the harbour with Capt. Horace Beaton at the helm. (MHF)

Hamonic Grief. Sad indeed, the cooling hulk of the once proud *Hamonic* is shown the day after the Point Edward waterfront was struck with tragedy. On 17 July 1945, fire spreading from the adjoining freight shed jumped to the moored ship, eventually destroying the vessel. Thanks to the quick action of Capt. Beaton and a nearby crane operator, all 400 passengers aboard were saved. The sad remains of a proud ship were towed to the Steel Company of Canada at Hamilton and scrapped during 1946. For weeks after the conflagration, debris from the fire floated down the St. Clair River, grim reminder of a soon to close chapter in upper lakes passenger service. (MHF)

Huronic. Perhaps the least known of the three Northern Navigation steamers because she was the first and oldest, yet the 1901-1902-built combined freighter-passenger vessel also had her day. When the *Noronic* came along the *Huronic* was put in a lesser role and by the 1930s was running in freight service only. In fact later years saw the cabins removed to allow for additional storage room. The *Huronic* ran until the end of the 1949 season, the *Noronic* disaster perhaps hastening her demise. Shown at the Point Edward freight shed docks sometime during the 1930s, *Huronic* (built in Collingwood) went under her own power in 1949 to Hamilton where the veteran ship was scrapped to end the story of the three sisters *Huronic, Hamonic* and *Noronic* in upper lakes passenger service. (MHF)

Look Dear! Excited passengers aboard this Northern Navigation steamer are not only enjoying the cool lake breezes but are observng an oncoming ship. When the open waters of the lakes are travelled, the hearty stay on deck and build up a good appetite. In the spacious parlour, card games, socializing and letter writing take up most of the leisure time. The dinner bell however brings everyone to alert. The *Noronic, Hamonic* and earlier on *Huronic* offered outstanding service for travellers. (MHF)

Departure Euphoria. Boundless excitement and anticipation awaited the excursionists who gathered at the Northern Navigation dock at Point Edward during the first half of the 20th century. The three Canada Steamship sisters *Huronic, Hamonic* and *Noronic* offered stimulating cruises that brought patrons upbound to the head of the Great Lakes with stops at Port Arthur, Fort William and Duluth. Various travel packages were offered over the years, but generally the C.S.L. passenger steamers travelled between Windsor-Detroit in the south, north to the Lakehead with Sarnia-Point Edward the main terminus for arrivals and departures. Locking through at the Soo was a highlight while many onboard activities such as afternoon tea and bridge, shuffleboard, the exercise walk around the decks, masquerade night and the evening singsong were all popular. And of course the cuisine aboard the steamers was outstanding with a full view of the passing panorama from the dining salon. Voyages on the "inland seas" in the finest vessels afloat created memories for many that lasted a lifetime. (MHF)

North American Going South. Although difficult to tell the two Georgian Bay Line sisters apart, the *North American* with rectangular windows arranged horizontally along the mid section, is shown passing Marine City in 1957. Both were representatives of beauty and class, their prestige evident through their appearance and the beautiful, melancholy strain of their steam whistles, sounding like no others on the Great Lakes. The two vessels were traffic stoppers along both sides of the St. Clair River as they passed. They represent a romantic period on the Great Lakes, one that will never be duplicated. The *North American* ran from 1913 until 1963 and suffered a sad fate when the 280 ft. ship plunged to the bottom of the Atlantic on 13 September 1967 while being towed south for another use. (MHF)

South(Ern) Dining. Happy 1959 Detroit to Duluth passengers pose for Harry Wolfe's camera in the dining room of the Georgian Bay Line five-day overnighter *South American*. These cameos would be treasured for years to come, appropriate images remembering new friends, fine cuisine, a glorious holiday and a legendary Great Lakes ship. College students were hired as crew, the most talented to be entertainers during the evening variety show. The white-hulled vessel, resembling a huge yacht, sailed the Great Lakes until 1967. Friday was her day to be downbound in the St. Clair River just a few minutes behind the *Noronic*. (MHF)

The D-III. No slowdown for the *City of Detroit III* as the D & C liner speeds upbound past Port Lambton in 1943, oblivious to the "Drive Slowly" school sign. Cutting white water and spewing ink black smoke from two of her stacks, the Frank E. Kirby-designed paddle wheeler built in 1911 at Detroit was a palace on the water. With 477 staterooms and 21 parlors, the exquisitely appointed steamer was premier class in all respects. So elegant and regal, the thump, thump of her paddle wheels foretold the coming of the *D-III*, sure to draw eyes to the St. Clair on a Sunday afternoon passing upbound. In 1950 an era had ended and her engines were finished, but her days of glory will be long remembered. (George Lee Collection)

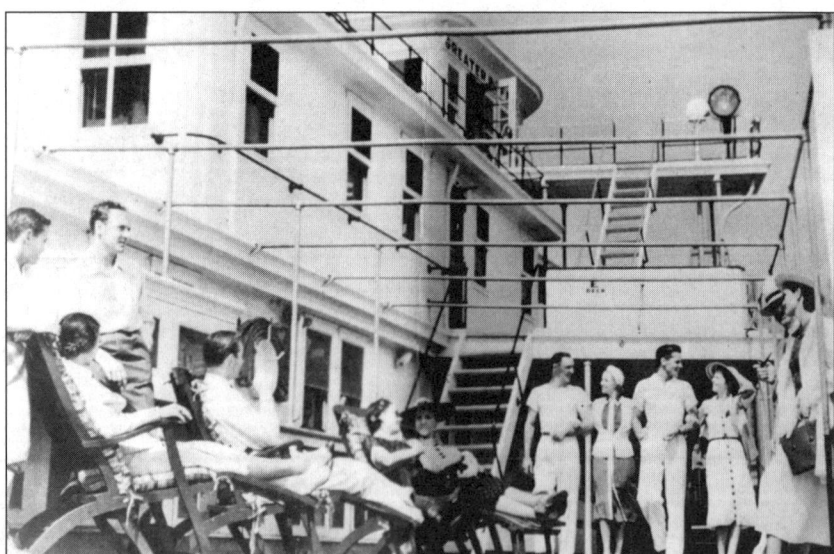

D & C The Grand Fleet. Passengers relax on deck near the bridge of the *Greater Detroit*, another of the Detroit & Cleveland Navigation fleet that adorned the Great Lakes. The *Greater Detroit* was launched 15 September 1923 at Detroit and was considered the ultimate in lakes travel. At 518 ft. and a power plant pushing the giant hull with 12,000 horsepower the vessel was capable of 21 knots. A sister ship *Greater Buffalo* was also built. With the auto taking over postwar and patronage declining in 1949, her final year of operation, the hull was painted white. But the end came in 1950 when the vessel was idled, and was purposely destroyed by fire in Lake St. Clair. (MHF)

River Crab Ride By. Whistle blow meets during the 1970s at Marine City, Marysville and St. Clair once again brought historic steam whistle sounds back to life. The 3 September 1979 conclave at Chuck Muer's River Crab Restaurant north of St. Clair was highlighted by the timely cruise-by of the historic Bob-Lo steamer *Columbia* on a special Detroit to Port Huron day trip. Whistles from many Great Lakes vessels including the famed *South American* were heard once again generating pleasant memories. (MHF)

Tashmoo Types. Esteemed Great Lakes historians and steam buffs, Andy Sykora and Frank Crevier admire the "whistle emeritus" from the famous St. Clair "flyer" *Tashmoo*. Brought to the River Crab meet by artist Jim Clary, re-creation of her sounds brought nostalgic tears to many present who had ridden her decks during her running years that ended in 1936. Similiar emotions were felt by sailors who heard ship sounds they thought would never be echoed again. (MHF)

DON'T MISS THE ALL DAY BOAT TRIP DETROIT TO PORT HURON

- 3 DATES -

MON. MAY 28th
WED. JULY 4th
MON. SEPT. 3rd

PRICE $9.00 ROUND TRIP

DEPART DETROIT 8:00 A.M.
RETURN DETROIT 7:00 P.M.

Bob-Lo's steamer Columbia will repeat the Port Huron trip that was so successful last year.

CRUISE THROUGH HISTORY

The water route is the one traveled more than two decades ago by such well known steamers as the Tashmoo, the Frank E. Kirby and the Western States. It takes the traveler across Lake St. Clair through the St. Clair Flats, world renowned as the "Venice of America," and up the St. Clair River past Harsens Island and Walpole Island with its Indian Reservation. There are the famous river towns of Marine City, St. Clair and Marysville and on the Canadian side, Ontario's "Chemical Valley."

DON'T DELAY

Tickets are $9 and may be obtained by mail from the Bob-Lo Company, 101 Woodward, Detroit, Mich. 48226, and Bob-Lo ticket office, foot of Woodward. Be sure you enclose a stamped, self-addressed envelope with your remittance.

SEE OTHER SIDE

Don't Miss It! When arrangements were made to charter a Bob-Lo steamer for three Detroit to Port Huron day trips during the 1979 season, the reaction was amazing. Many years had passed since the *Aquarama* or *Put-In-Bay* offered similar excursions, until this form of water transit was terminated in the 1960s. This presented a rare opportunity to duplicate the historic White Star route across Lake St. Clair, thorough the Venice of America, the St. Clair Flats area and upbound past the various communities on both sides of the St. Clair River. And what better perspective to enjoy the close up views of the many ships encountered during the day long trip. The 11-hour round trip made for a long day but afforded a unique experience. And the price was right at just $9.00, a steamboat bargain that must be seriously considered. And many did for the few seasons during the 1970s when an authentic steamboat ride could be had. (MHF)

High Hopes An anticipated return to the glory days of passenger service on the Great Lakes would begin once again when the *Aquarama* made an appearance on the Detroit River in 1955. Built in 1945 as a war vessel, the sleek and novel ship rated for 2500 passengers was put into service initially from Detroit to Cleveland. Day trips in the St. Clair River to Port Huron followed. However, postwar lifestyles saw people in a hurry driving their new DeSotos or Hudsons, and *Aquarama* was laid up at Muskegon in 1962. Many however can say they travelled on this ship that was mastered by the lakes legend Capt. Morgan Howell who was licensed to sail nearly all seas in the world. The 529 ft., 9900 horsepower ship languished for several years. Mild excitement surfaced in 1987 when new plans for the ship were announced. Again with Capt Howell on the bridge *Aquarama* was towed to Sarnia where the vessel, still fully equipped, was opened to the public for inspection. However the novelty eventually diminished and the former *Marine Star* was moored briefly at Marysville then moved to Windsor and finally to Buffalo where she remains with a dubious future hovering over the once busy ship. Shown are deck views of the *Aquarama* during better days. (John Flick)

Put-In-Bay. Another Frank Kirby design, this day steamer was built in 1911 at Wyandotte for Ashley & Dustin Steamship for the Detroit to Sandusky route. A fine dance floor was crowded with couples jiving and gliding to great dance orchestras. After many years on the Lake Erie route, alternate days saw the 226 ft. steamer on the St. Clair River Wednesday and Sunday afternoons for cruises to Port Huron. With work scarce during ensuing years the *Put-In-Bay* made a rare charter inland to Wallaceburg on 13 August 1951. Sadly at the end of the 1953 season the vessel was finished and on October 3rd of that year she was towed to Lake St. Clair where her upper decks were purposely burned, an unjust end for such a glorious ship. (MHF)

D & C. Such wonderful trips! Such glorious boats! Brimming with smoke, smacking the waters with their huge paddlewheels, decks streaming with happy travellers heading to such places as Buffalo, Mackinac Island, Chicago and all those other dream destinations. When they tied up at Detroit in 1950 an elegant era was over. Their memories were many as they had played such an important role in Great Lakes history. (MHF)

Four
Brief Visitors
Short Stay Ships

Wolverine. Word circulated in August of 1942 that something special was to pass upbound in the St. Clair River. The river was very busy in those days but as soon as this strange sight appeared abreast of Walpole Island, special attention was directed to the river. The former *Seeandbee* "the largest sidewheeler in the world" had been converted to a training aircraft carrier at Buffalo and was heading to Lake Michigan for duty. Launched in 1912, the *Seeandbee* had passed through the St. Clair River during runs to Mackinac Island and other northern points. As an aircraft carrier she performed well and once retired in August of 1945 was idled and scrapped at Milwaukee in 1947. *Wolverine* is shown on 19 August 1942, the date the former queen was on the St. Clair River. (MHF)

Sainte Marie in St. Clair. Spending almost her entire career as spare boat to the *Chief Wawatam*, the Mackinac Transportation Co. rail ferry *Sainte Marie (2)* was built at Toledo in 1913 for service in the Straits of Mackinac area. Due to her strong hull the vessel was suited for ice breaking and was hired on occasion by the Lake Carriers Association. Mrs. Mabel Smith, operator of the Red & White General Store in Port Lambton, snapped this photo of *Sainte Marie (2)* breaking heavy ice opposite her place of business. This extremely rare view was deemed significant and Mrs. Smith had postcards made to sell in her store. *Sainte Marie (2)* capable of carrying 14 rail cars, was sold for scrapping at Ashtabula in 1961, her fourth trip on the St. Clair River going to her final destination. (MHF)

Royal Yacht. The St. Clair River became "Royal Row" briefly as Queen Elizabeth and Prince Philip made their 1959 Great Lakes tour in the royal yacht *Britannia*. The splendid vessel launched on 16 April 1953 drew thousands of spectators on both sides of the St. Clair River during the upbound trip, much like a wave as interested spectators followed along the river until *Britannia* was out of sight in Lake Huron. The hype and excitement was lacking when the *Britannia* (without the royal couple) was on her return trip, shown in the St. Clair River in July of 1959. The royal yacht was decommissioned December 1997 and has been turned into a museum ship at Edinburgh. (Bill Abraham)

Dodge's Delphine. Every once in a while residents along the St. Clair River would catch a glimpse of one of the most elegant vessels ever viewed on the waterway. If upbound the *Delphine* (built in 1921 at Ecorse for $2,000,000) was either on a short jaunt or heading for the North Channel in Georgian Bay. Horace Dodge of car fame had the yacht built for his wife Anna but he died before it was completed. Taken over during the Second World War it was renamed *USS Dauntless* but was returned to the Dodge family after the war. Following Anna Dodge's death the elegant vessel passed through various ownerships. During 2006 a several-year restoration was completed overseas and the remarkable vessel is available for charter in Brugge, Belgium. *Delphine* is shown in 1950 in the St. Clair River near Courtright. (MHF)

St. Heliers. A former Canadian government buoy tender, the *St. Heliers* was purchased by JAL Steamship Co. of Wallaceburg in 1960, spending the winter there at the C & D Sugar Co. wharf. Sold to a Panama company and renamed *Tropic Seas*, the vessel became internationally known when a murder took place on the deck in the Caribbean. The story along with other questionable escapades hit the front cover of Canada's weekly magazine, *Macleans*. As *Inland Seas*, the vessel is shown passing through the Lord Selkirk Bridge on the Sydenham River, 6 November 1960 heading to her winter berth. The following spring an amateur crew delivered the vessel to Toronto handing her over to new owners. (MHF)

Seldom Seen. Built in 1952 at Montreal as *Frankcliffe Hall (1)* for Halco, this canaller was an infrequent visitor to the St. Clair River as most of her time was spent in the St. Lawrence River. In 1962 her name was changed to *Northcliffe Hall* and soon the 259 ft. bulker was working in the Caribbean before returning to the Great Lakes in 1976 and being given her pictured name *Roland Desgagnes*. She is shown in the Port Huron area, 2 November 1980. Two years later she sank in the St. Lawrence River. (Dick Wicklund Collection)

Strange Waters. Generally at home in Lake Michigan, the Grand Trunk rail ferry *City of Milwaukee* is downbound in 1978 in the St. Clair River nearing Port Lambton. Due to some labour disruption she was forced to the lower lakes for some required work at Lorain. Built in 1931 to carry both rail cars and passengers, the ship was coal fired until 1947 when converted to oil. When Grand Trunk's service terminated in 1978 she was chartered to do the Kewaunee to Frankfurt run which lasted only briefly. Attempts are underway to preserve the classic ship as a museum on Lake Michigan. (George Lee Collection)

Calypso and Cousteau. Small but functional and certainly famous, the *Calypso* with world famous explorer Jacques Cousteau and his crew, made a well documented trip into the Great Lakes in the summer of 1980. The *Calypso* is on her outbound trip, passing through the St. Clair River south of Marine City. The mariners drew wide attention from the media as they explored the world's largest freshwater system. Special pilot aboard the *Calypso* during her St. Clair River trip was legendary Great Lakes veteran Capt. Morgan Howell who was licensed to sail most waters of the world. Although looking trim in the photo, later years saw the *Calypso* lying derelict in France, her future in question. (George Lee Collection)

Dana T. Bowen. Spending most of her career in the upper lakes, the handsome tug *Dana T. Bowen* is shown on the Chenal Ecarte River at Port Lambton during winter layup, 22 December 1972. Built in 1938 at Sorel as *Magpie* and used by the Abitibi Power & Paper Co. the lovely diesel tug was purchased by Capt. George Hindman in 1966 and renamed *Dana T. Bowen* in honour of a dear family friend and renowned writer of Great Lakes history. The 100 ft. tug was surplus, purchased by Lee Marine in 1972 who in turn sold the vessel to J.W. Purvis Marine in 1972, and she sails as *W.J. Ivan Purvis*. (MHF)

Canadian Franko. Seldom seen in the St. Clair River area until a brief stay in 1977, this handsome tug was built at Owen Sound in 1944 as *Glenlivet II* for the Royal Canadian Navy. She passed through various postwar ownerships until coming to the St. Clair River area named *Canadian Franko* in 1977. Owned by Frank Rawlings of Chatham the tug had been converted to private use as a pleasure craft. Shown passing through the channel between Fawn Island and the mainland (near the Southwestern Sales dock) she was sold again and sails under the name *Vigilant I*. (George Lee Collection)

INLAND SEAS. Originally built in 1943 as a mine layer, post war this wooden hull was in use at Isle Royal, named *Ranger II*. The University of Michigan was next owner, using the vessel as a research and study on-water laboratory. In 1973 she was purchased by Lee Marine of Port Lambton, then sold three years later to Leonard Putney in Connecticut and used briefly as a whale watching ship. *Inland Seas* is now landlocked in Carleton, Quebec converted to a restaurant. (George Lee Collection)

GLOBAL STAR. Drawing curious eyes in the St. Clair River, this small but luxurious passenger excursion vessel was built in Denmark as a hospital ship in 1955 named *Missigsut*. She served in Greenland until 1977 when purchased by John McGoff. It was during this period *Global Star* was seen briefly in the St. Clair River area and was in layup for a period at the Lee Marine dock in Port Lambton. After leaving the area she became a dive charter yacht in the Caribbean area. (George Lee Collection)

ASSINIBOIA. The sleek Canadian Pacific passenger vessel made only one previous appearance in the St. Clair River, when she was "on her way to work" after coming over from Scotland in 1908. Here she is shown at Point Edward in 1968 following her retirement. The classic and beautifully appointed 346 ft. vessel spent her career running from Port McNicholl to the Lakehead. Retirement came in 1967 and the vessel was purchased by JAL Steamship under Donald Lee of Port Lambton. In August of 1968 under her own power she headed to Philadelphia for restaurant use but unfortunately was destroyed by fire there 11 November 1969. A sister ship *Keewatin* survives in Douglas, Michigan as a museum. (George Lee Collection)

ANNANDALE. This 1967 Norwegian-built vessel once picked up *NASA* nose cones and was also used by Jacques Cousteau in 1991. John McGoff of Lansing purchased the former research vessel and the 90 footer spent some time in the St. Clair River area in the 1970s. Shown docked at Port Lambton, she was purchased by Capt. Wm. Hoey of Detroit area and following another sale went to South America as a missionary vessel. (George Lee Collection)

HIDING STARS? - During the late 1980s and early 1990s "Star" ships, *Star of Detroit, Chicago, Chicago I and II*, started appearing in the lower St. Clair River usually docked either at Lee Marine in Port Lambton north or on the Chenal Ecarte at the McMillan Marine dock. Idled and temporarily out of work, the vessels moored during speculation discussions as to their future. In the meantime they brought inquisitive glances from observers pondering their fate and future. Shown 7 August 1991 on the Chenal Ecarte are the *Star of Chicago* and larger *Star of Detroit*. (MHF)

STAR OF DETROIT. Arriving at the Lee Marine dock Port Lambton earlier that season *Star of Detroit*, a sleek handsome day boat is shown 21 November 1987 preparing for winter layup. In a market that was flexible, the dinner cruise business seemed to go in cycles often tapering off once the novelty seemed to diminish. *Star of Detroit* was built in 1984 by Chesepeake Shipbuilding at Salisbury, Maryland. At 165 ft., capable of hosting 625, after a brief stay in the St. Clair area she left in 1992 was renamed and is on the east coast. (MHF)

NEW YORK BOUND. The *"Sen. John J. Marchi"* was the second of three Staten Island ferries to pass down the St. Clair River after construction by Marinette (Wisconsin) Marine, along with the first *Guy V. Molinari*. The *Spirit of America* passed downbound in the St. Clair River in September of 2005. The bright orange hulls created excitement upon their brief but spectacular appearances on the way to New York. The pictured *Sen. John J. Marchi* passed down the St. Clair River in November of 2005. (Gerry Ouderkirk Collection)

CHI-CHEEMAUN. No, the 1974-built car and passenger ferry didn't make a wrong turn from her accustomed Tobermory-South Baymouth route! During the winter of 2005-2006 Sarnia is her base as the massive 365 ft. vessel undergoes mechanical refurbishing. The big white hull spans the entire width of Sarnia's inner harbour her stern nudging the *Mississagi* that was enjoying a brief winter stay. The *Chi-Cheemaun* became a tourist attraction to the Sarnia waterfront and is scheduled to return in late 2006 for further work. The vessel resumed her Georgian Bay route in time to start the new season in May. (MHF)

Five
Booms & Piles
Mountain Makers

THE FORKS. Where the Sydenham River ends and meets the Chenal Ecarte at a juncture called "Forks" the river gods had a habit of building up the mud thus impeding passing ships particularly those of deep draught. Thus every three or four years it was necessary to remove the sediment. The steam barge *Ontario* owned by the Chatham Dredging Co. often was given the task of clearing the channel. An unidentified tall stack tug is standing by during this operation sometime in the late 1920s. (MHF)

MUD SLINGING. Unloading of another kind comes when silting channels require dredging in inland waters used for shipping. The rather slow moving Sydenham River was notorious for throwing new shoals in the path of unsuspecting vessels. The steam barge *Eleanor* and tug *Champlain* of Sin Mac Lines are busy clearing a sand bar in the Sydenham River at the Forks (where the Chenal Ecarte continues its way to Lake St. Clair.) Time is 1930s. (MHF)

BAYGEORGE. Tucked away and framed in foliage, this vessel unloading coal at Wallaceburg's H.J. Heinz plant in July of 1964, started out life as a tanker. Built in 1912 as *Iocoma* for Imperial Oil she served that company for 40 years. In 1951 a complete conversion to a bulker took place at Montreal preparing the vessel for a new role. By 1961 the vessel was named *Baygeorge* and the 248 ft. self unloader could easily negotiate inland destinations. Serving well, her final chapter came in 1971 when the once busy vessel was scrapped at Hamilton. (MHF)

WEED CUTTER?. The venerable *Alpena* of the Wyandotte Transportation Co. seems to be caught in a weed field but still has her engines up. No, the 1909-built self unloader (second ever built on the Great Lakes) is just fine as she is carefully feeling her way along the Chenal Ecarte in 1954 seeking the Southwestern Sales Co. dock to unload some gravel. Even though the channel is narrow, the water is deep and this trip as many others to the same dock went with smooth routine. (MHF)

TIGHT SQUEEZE. For several seasons in the 1950s McQueen Marine tug *Patricia McQueen* towed the barge *T.F. Newman* through the narrow Chenal Ecarte and Sydenham Rivers to Wallaceburg where coal was unloaded at the Daniels Co. dock along the east branch of the river. It was a rather tricky and tight squeeze but the several trips made the practice perfect. The *Newman* and *McQueen* are shown nearing the dock in October of 1954 with a cargo of 1400 T of coal to be unloaded. The barge ended up as a dock face at the Canadian Soo. (MHF)

BEN W. CALVIN. What a good looker! That line of forward port holes and extended bridge combine for a regal appearance. The vessel came out in 1911 as *William C. Agnew* at Lorain and sailed under that name as a straight decker until 1926 when renamed *George F. Rand* still with American Steamship. By 1954 she had gained her pictured name. During her career as a self unloader which began in 1936 the vessel was a frequent visitor to the St. Clair River until 1974 when a productive career had terminated. She was scrapped in Spain during 1974 another loss to the Great Lakes. (Fr. Vanderlinden - Moran Collection)

BUCKEYE (2). Launched at Cleveland 29 January 1910 as the straight decker *Leonard B. Miller* the vessel was perhaps best known in her latter years because she held out so long competing with much larger and modern ships. By 1921 the vessel was in Columbia colours and given new name *Charles W. Galloway* in 1937 and by 1958 was converted to a combined self unloader crane ship with another name *Robert C. Norton*. The *Buckeye* phase came in 1974 and until she stopped running by herself in 1979 became well known among avid ship watchers due to her triple chime whistle and unique styling complete with two large deck cranes. She became a barge for awhile but lost much of her appeal and was scrapped in 1994. (Fr. Vanderlinden - Moran Collection)

MADE IN ST. CLAIR! - Another large "build" by the Great Lakes Engineering Co. in St. Clair, was the pictured *Avondale* that came out in 1908 as the *Adam E. Cornelius (1)* with an overall length of 440 ft. In 1942 an extra 49 ft. in length was added at Manitowoc plus a self unloader. After two more name changes *Detroit Edison (1)* in 1948 and *George F. Rand (2)* in 1954, the vessel was picked up by Reoch Steamship 1962 and enjoyed a few more years of work. Only the astute knew the vessel was built in St. Clair as she passed by that community many times in her career. Simply worn out by 1975 her career had terminated and this glorious old ship had done her duty. Scrapping in Spain came in 1979. (Fr.Vanderlinden - Moran Collection)

FINAL PASS BY. Sailing routinely past Port Huron 21 November 1974, the Algoma Central Railway self unloader *Roy A. Jodrey* is heading to the lower lakes unaware of the unkind fate awaiting the vessel. Launched at Collingwood 9 November 1965, the attractive 640 ft. vessel had performed routinely to this point. Dick Wicklund captured this great view and was somewhat taken when he heard that less than two weeks later the *Jodrey* was gone. On November 20 the vessel ran aground in the St. Lawrence River near Alexandria Bay, N.Y., and sank the next day in 150 ft., of water, fortunately with no loss of life but the loss of a very young vessel. (Dick Wicklund Collection)

SLOAN IN TROUBLE. On 16 April 1990 the *George A. Sloan* slipped by Port Huron with tugs at both bow and stern. One of three "maritimers" built during the second world war the 620 ft. vessel came out in 1943 and would be a most dependable vessel for Pittsburgh and U.S. Steel who put the vessel in the iron ore trade. It was unusual to see the *George A. Sloan* under assistance as she sailed most effectively and routinely for so many years. The Great Lakes tugs *Superior* and *Missouri* are in charge as they tow the disabled vessel for repairs at a lower lakes repair dock. Sad to see her leave U.S. Steel colours but elated she had more life, the *Sloan* became *Mississagi* for Lower Lakes Towing in 2001 and usually spends the winter in layup in Sarnia. (Dick Wicklund Collection)

RECORS POINT. The huge Detroit Edison power plant north of Marine City relies upon self unloaders to feed her furnaces with coal. Seldom does a day go by without a ship in sight at the plant. The fall is particularly busy as stockpiling is carried out before winter ice prevents navigation. From the Canadian shoreline, a wonderful broadside perspective of ships unloading at the Recors Point is enjoyed. Shown is the *John J. Boland,* one of three ships to bear that name unloading coal at the Detroit Edison plant in 1957. (Carl Cramer Collection)

ARE YOU SINKING? - Sitting very low in St. Clair River waters, the familiar sandsucker *K.V. Schwartz* bustles along the lower portion of the river in 1950. This low profile was typical of the venerable vessel usually loaded to the hilt after sucking sand from the river bottom. She served a most remarkable life, built way back in 1884 starting as a package freighter named *Syracuse*. Tossed around over the years like a hot potato, the vessel experienced several ownerships and even spent a spell carrying passengers based in Port Huron. Under the name *Lakewood,* the 267 ft. vessel became a sand dredge and during this particular period served mainly in the eastern end of Lake Ontario. In 1947 *Lakewood* came to Detroit and was converted to a self unloader, her name now *K.V. Schwartz*. Remaining years would be spent in the St. Clair River area taking on the name *Algonac* in 1953. She even ventured inland to Wallaceburg on several occasions. A most faithful performer, the end came in 1975 after 90 years of service *Algonac*, a friend of the St. Clair area was scrapped at Toledo. (MHF)

JOHN T. HUTCHINSON. Carrying the "Hutchinson" name meant longevity on the Great Lakes and in the case of the *John T.*, reprieve from fate. Launched at Lorain in 1927 as *George M. Humphrey*, the 586 ft. ship sailed peacefully until 15 June 1943 when she collided with the *D.M. Clemson* in the Straits of Mackinac and sank. Given up by Kinsman Transit her owners, she was eventually salvaged by Capt. John Roen, sailing for 42 more years. The vessel is entering the St. Clair River in September of 1978. (MHF)

A.M. BYERS. Upbound at Marine City this Reiss vessel was built in 1910 at Cleveland first serving as a straight decker for the first 45 years with a self unloader added in 1955 at Toledo. A frequent visitor to the St. Clair River, her name was changed to *Clemens Reiss* and then *Jack Wirt* in 1970. After 63 years of good service the end came in 1973, another classic self unloader out competed by the new and larger vessels that gradually pushed most of the veterans aside. (MHF)

Six
War Route
Gray with Guns

H.M.C.S. WALLACEBURG. A steady parade of wartime Great Lakes-built ships were seen downbound in the St. Clair River during the early stage of the 1939-1945 conflict. Conveniently, the pictured algerine class minesweeper, launched at Port Arthur in 1943, was allowed a two day stay at her namesake port of Wallaceburg. Before heading to the war zone, a ceremonial breaking of a champagne bottle over her bow was officiated by the wife of Wallaceburg's mayor. The vessel was also open for public tours during the stay and the crew was showered with gifts including a piano. (MHF)

H.M.C.S. ORILLIA. Making just one brief (downbound) trip on the St. Clair River, the pictured minesweeper was one of the many on the outbound trip during world war two. Collingwood Shipbuilding Co. helped the Allied cause by turning out 24 vessels, 14 corvettes for the Royal Canadian Navy, 8 for the British Navy and 3 for the U.S. Navy. The pictured *H.M.C.S. Orillia* launched in November 1940 served in the North Atlantic convoy escort service and was scrapped in 1951. (MHF)

H.M.C.S. SARNIA. This bangor class minesweeper was commissioned in Toronto 13 August 1942. Although never appearing in the St. Clair River, this war vessel carried Sarnia's name throughout the conflict, city citizens proud of this representation. Serving in Atlantic convoy duty, the ship was instrumental in rescuing survivors of the doomed *H.M.C.S. Esquimault*. The *H.M.C.S. Sarnia* served until 1972 after 14 years with the Turkish Navy. (MHF)

H.M.C.S. NOOTKA (2). May of 1963 saw another Royal Canadian Navy visitor when the tribal class destroyed *H.M.C.S. Nootka (2)* was upbound in the St. Clair River. Shown passing Port Lambton this vessel was commissioned at Halifax 7 August 1946 and served initially as a training ship in the Caribbean until conversion to a destroyer escort in 1949. Upon return to Halifax at the end of 1952, she had gained the distinction of being only the second RCN vessel to circumnavigate the globe. After this 1963 Great Lakes tour, the ship was retired and paid off at Halifax 6 February 1964 and broken up in Scotland the next year. (MHF)

H.M.C.S. FUNDY – No. 159 was the third vessel of the Royal Canadian Navy to carry this name. Commissioned at Lauzon, Quebec 19 March 1954 as a post war minesweeper, the vessel was on a Great Lakes goodwill tour in 1961, stopping at Wallaceburg where her Capt. Lt. Cdr. James Butterfield was able to visit relatives. The vessel also made a stop at Sarnia during the tour. (MHF)

BOLD VENTURE – September of 1963 brought a prominent second war veteran to the Great Lakes when the former *H.M.C.S. Brockville*, commissioned in Sorel 19 September 1942 sailed up the St. Clair River and surprisingly headed inland at Walpole Island entering the Chenal Ecarte River. After being paid off by the Royal Canadian Navy, as a surplus ship the vessel was purchased by JAL Steamship Co. of Wallaceburg renaming the vessel *Bold Venture*. Drawing surprises all along the inland route, the former minesweeper negotiated the narrow waterway passage and moored in Wallaceburg where flocks of locals headed to the waterfront to hail her arrival. The vessel wintered over 1963 and 1964 in Wallaceburg the first war ship - ever known to be in that position in a community known for glass making. The *Bold Venture* is on her inbound trip on the Chenal Ecarte nearing the Dark Bend, just a few miles from her mooring in Wallaceburg. (MHF)

PORTE DAUPHINE. With pendant number 186, this Royal Canadian Navy auxiliary vessel was launched at Pictou, Nova Scotia 24 April 1952. Designed as a gate keeper ship, the vessel spent much of her time as a research vessel. During a Great Lakes tour in the summer of 1975, *H.M.C.S. Porte Dauphine* came to the port of Wallaceburg as part of the town's centennial celebration and is shown moored in that community 30 June 1975. (MHF)

THE JAL OFFICIALS. Donald Lee, left and Alfred Benn, right with Lyle Lapointe, guest chief engineer aboard the *Bold Venture* confer on deck pondering their next move. Lee and Benn formed the steamship company hoping to develop a future for the former minesweeper. With lots of power, an experienced Lakes pilot was required so former Colonial Steamship *Mathewston* captain and local resident Ray Kidd took the helm during the *Bold Venture's* inland trip. After various proposals, JAL Steamship accepted an offer for purchase in December of 1964 that saw the former minesweeper head to Montreal for use in connection with EXPO '67 a huge celebration in connection with Canada's 100th birthday. Wallaceburg's brief but significant love affair with a war vessel was one to remember. (MHF)

H.M.C.S. HAIDA. This Canadian war hero was the last of 27 tribal class destroyers built during World War 2. Shown visiting Sarnia from May 17 to 21 1963 during a Canadian Navy Veterans reunion, the ship was decommissioned in 1963. Built in England during 1943 her meritorious service was rewarded by being restored as a museum ship at Ontario Place in Toronto beginning in 1971. After several years of thousands touring her every nook and cranny, in August of 2005 the historic vessel was transferred to Hamilton where she continued to represent an important segment of Canada's second world war legacy. (Alvon Jackson Collection)

H.M.C.S. OTTAWA. Shown at the Sarnia government wharf 22 May 1992, the pictured war vessel *H.M.C.S. Ottawa* stopped as part of an extensive farewell tour throughout the Great Lakes. The third Canadian warship to hold this name, *No. 229* was built at Montreal and commissioned 21 October 1964. After the vessel departed Sarnia in May of 1992, the relatively modern destroyer escort headed to Montreal for refitting. On 31 July 1992, *H.M.C.S. Ottawa* was decommissioned. (MHF)

Seven
Pleasure Plus
Speed with Class

WHERE IT ALL BEGAN. Christopher Columbus Smith and his brother Henry loved the St. Clair Flats and began building duckboats about 1874. Their design was popular which led to the eventual establishment of C.S. & H.M. Smith Co. forerunner of Chris Craft Corporation the world's largest producers of pleasure craft. Algonac was the home of this mega corporation that grew to be an international concern. The economy of Algonac was built on the Smith family enterprise that began on a modest basis. Runabouts, cruisers and even small kit boats and prams plus items such as water skis and gun cabinets were produced by the company. A 1927 "Vacation Days Ahead" advertisement shows two of the open runabouts offered that year, a 26 ft. model guaranteed to go 40 miles per hour could be purchased for $4,000. The Chris Craft logo that changed a number of times was stylized to the familiar script that represents a prestigious hall mark, with hundreds of the Chris Craft products lovingly cared for today, highly valued for their antiquity. (MHF)

1927 Chris-Craft advertisement in *National Geographic*

SPEED AND GRACE – As Chris Smith, company founder, would rather hunt or fish during his later years, operation of the Algonac plant was passed along to his sons. Offsprings Chris, Jay, Bernard and Owen (Socks) ran the operation after their father died in 1939. By the year 1940 Chris Craft had enjoyed one of the best sales years ever. The 1938 15.5 ft. utility runabout and the pictured Chris Craft Challenger (shown is a 1941) model were amongst the best sellers. However, war was underway overseas and Chris Craft knew they would be involved, confirmed after Pearl Harbor in December of 1941. Swinging over to war production the company joined the fray by building army command boats, landing craft, aircraft rescue boats and other products that eventually won the firm the coveted *"Army-Navy E Award"* for proficiency. With a changing market, Algonac was shocked when Chris Craft corporate offices were moved to Pompano Beach, Florida in 1957, but the name Chris Craft would we strongly connected to the St. Clair River community for many years to come. (MHF)

THE CRAFT WAS CONTAGIOUS. Although Chris Craft Corporation was the giant (and world's largest) numerous other smaller boat building enterprises would spring up in the St. Clair River area. Undeterred by the big neighbour practically next door. Dr. C. Eckfield, a naval architect, started a boat building company in 1925 at Algonac. Specializing in both inboard and outboards, the Eckfield Boat Co. produced for a few years but was hit by the depression during the late 1920s and was forced to close in 1930. However the smaller producer was never questioned as to quality. (MHF)

Describing the 1959 Mariner 20' Typhoon

MARINER AT MARINE CITY. With unlimited choice of waterways in the St. Clair area, it was not a surprise that another pleasure boat builder appeared on the scene in the 1950s. Mariner Boat Co. started in a former roller rink at Roberts Landing and moved to Marine City in 1958. With a wide beam, the Mariners rode well and gained a top notch reputation as a good alternate to the big company located further south on the St. Clair River. A number of Mariner boats have managed to survive, products from the company that ceased operations in the 1960s. (MHF)

CLASSIC BEAUTY. Palatial yachts such as the one pictured at Highbanks Park at Walpole Island were a mark of distinction during earlier times. The *Pryun* was an 88 ft. classic that spent a lot of time in the Algonac area as well as the extent of the St. Clair area from her home port in Wallaceburg. The Lee family acquired *Pryun* in 1914 and operated the vessel for a number of years before selling the 1900 Bay City-built beauty to Capt. Frank Craighe of Fort William in 1918. (MHF)

RACING FEVER. Both inboard and outboard races gained popularity after the second world war. With time to play and money to spend, racing fever took hold at Algonac, Wallaceburg, Marine City, Sarnia and other spots in the St. Clair area. Special holidays such as Dominion Day (July 1) in Canada and 4th of July celebrations in the U.S. were times for races while Marine City held outboard races during their annual summer festival. Shown is a 1 July 1946 unlimited boat race held during Dominion Day celebrations in Wallaceburg. The course is ringed by visiting yachters from the Detroit Yacht Club. (MHF)

MISS CHEVROLET. Following the second world war many surplus vessels were made available to the public by both the U.S. and Canadian governments. A convenient size for conversion to private use were wood hull fairmiles, 112 ft. vessels that were employed in coastal duties and surveillance. Six of this class were built by Mac-Craft in Sarnia during the war. A prime example of a conversion was *Q-107* built by Grew Boats in Penetanguishene, Ontario, the hull commissioned 11 September 1943. While under the pictured name the vessel was owned by Chester Ferris of Sarnia and is shown visiting Wallaceburg in June of 1949. (MHF)

HOME BUILT TOO. With a large pool of marine carpenters, many who were employed in the St. Clair area production centres, both sides of the border, boasted skilled home craft builders. Ranging from small row boats to cruisers and also assembling of kit boats, the area waters found a strong mix with production models. Shown is one such example hitting the water for the first time. Spring of 1965 saw the launching at Wallaceburg of a small cruiser built by former Mac-Craft worker Eric Morse (at the bow) and Bob Hunter (far left) while Doug McLean and Omar VanWatteghem assisting. Many of these home built varieties were every bit as reliable as the more expensive production models, a testimony to the skill, of the amateur craftsmen. (MHF)

WORLD CLASS EVENT. The most prestigious sporting event held in the St. Clair River area came in September of 1933. The legendary Gar Wood had been challenged by Britisher Hubert Scott-Paine for world unlimited powerboat supremacy with the famed Harmsworth trophy at stake. The local hero from Algonac, Gar Wood in his *Miss America X* was rivalled by Paine's *Miss Britain III* powered by a 12 cylinder airplane engine. The hype built up for the 25 nautical mile course laid out between Marine City and Roberts Landing was unprecedented. Held over a three day period (September 2, 4 and 5) Gar Wood in his sleek mahogany displacement hull had four engines that delivered a whopping combined 6,400 horsepower, Mechanic Orland Johnson shown with Gar Wood left was at his side. Marine architect Napoleon Lisee from Marine City played an important part as well. The sleek speed boat hull is shown prepping for the race at Algonac prior to the event. With the Union Jack their flag at the time, viewers on the Canadian shoreline tended to cheer for Scott-Paine. (MHF)

CASH COW EVENT? Communities on both sides of the Harmsworth Race course hoped to cash in on the influx of visitors from around the world. Food concessions, parking lots, accommodation sites, souvenir sales and even selling of special edition newspapers were schemes to capture the crowds. Make shift bleacher seats were set up at Sombra, the Minnie and McRitchie families two of the entrepreneurs. Unfortunately (and unforeseen) the race course was effectively blocked off from good Canadian viewing spots by the hundreds of steamboats and pleasure craft that anchored in the St. Clair River. The spectacular air view (with Gar Wood leading) shows the view blockade rendering east bank viewers inferior vantage spots. Although a valiant effort by Hubert Scott-Paine was put forth, engine failure was his downfall and Gar Wood successfully defended his title. (MHF)

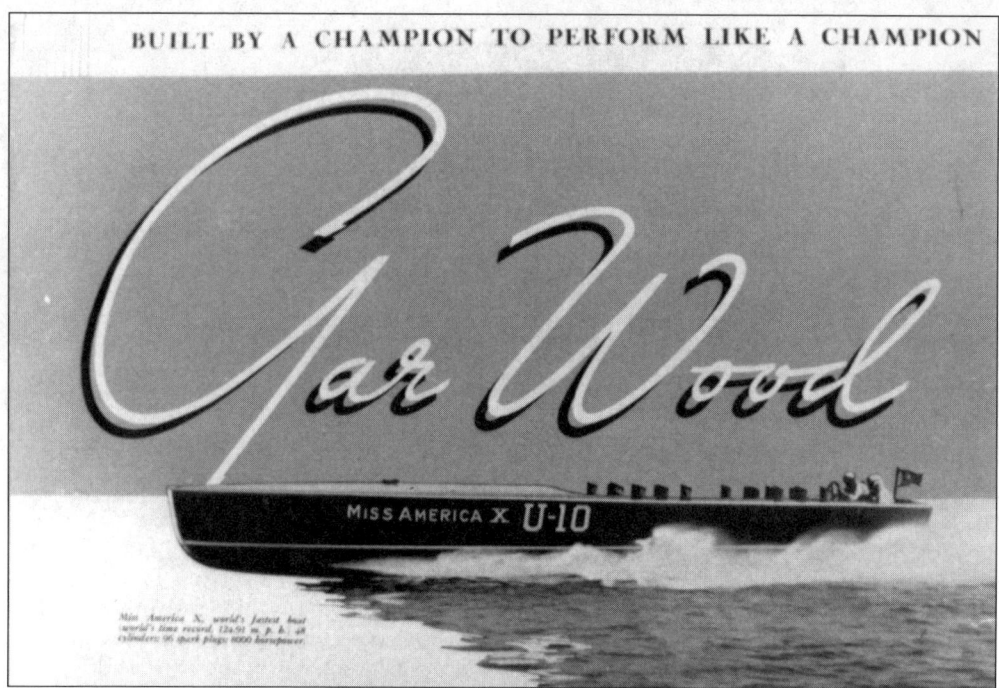

GAR WOOD. With his lucrative patent of the hydraulic lift, Garfield Wood branched into his first love, boating. First at Algonac, he went into the production of fine pleasure boats making his mark with what would be considered by many as representing the finest in workmanship. His racing boats, built in sequence with the name *Miss America* were equally judged with high quality. In 1930 he left Algonac and built an ultra modern plant upriver at Marysville, south of Port Huron where production on a much larger scale continued. Fine craft ranging from 16 to 32 ft. were built at this new plant which stood on the banks of the St. Clair River. (MHF)

1932 view of Gar Wood plant at Marysville on the banks of St. Clair River

MASS PRODUCTION. An interior view of the Gar Wood plant shows the immensity of production levels. The Algonac plant was rather primitive in comparison to the modern techniques employed when the new Marysville operation was underway in 1930. Interest in pre-war Gar Wood built craft is high amongst antique boat collectors. In order to share information, a very active Gar Wood Antique Boat Club exists with members in North America numbering in the hundreds. When the long lost Gar Wood plant records were uncovered, this made study of production much easier and provided answers for many previously unsolved questions. The 1937 16 ft. custom runabout is one of the many examples showing the high craftsman standards expected. During the second war, Gar Wood switched over to assist through the production (beginning in 1942) of close to 200 craft ranging from 33 ft. to 46 ft. including picket, tow, target and plane personnel boats. (MHF)

1937 Gar Wood 16' Custom Runabout

Canadian "Wild Cat," Queen of the Waters

1927 24' "Wild Cat" Runabout
45 M.P.H. 150 H.P. Scripps....$4000.00   40 M.P.H., 100 H.P. Scripps....$3250.00

The World's Finest and Fastest Pleasure Craft
Made in Ontario

NO summer home on the water is complete without a Canadian "Wild Cat." The most beautiful boat made. Their upper lines are keen and striking, with running lines that speak for themselves when you "give her the gun" and pass boats having 50 per cent. more power.

Designed and built in perfect balance, and driven through a gear box with propeller shaft nearly in same plane of boat's travel.
They straighten out on the water in place of running up hill. That's why a seven-passenger, 24-foot Wild Cat runs better than 40 miles per hour with a 100 H.P. motor.

ONTARIO BOAT & ENGINE WORKS
WALLACEBURG, ONTARIO
BUILDERS OF THE
Famous Baby "Wild Cat" Jr.

CANADIAN CONTENT. Within the St. Clair area were Canadian producers of pleasure boats. In 1927, Algonac resident Jack Beebe came to Wallaceburg and established the Ontario Boat & Engine Works. Production was modelled after Henry Ford's assembly line method, the Canadian company growing quickly to make the claim as the country's first producers of that type. Boats were on display at shows in Toronto and New York and were well received especially the 24 ft. Wild Cat runabout with highly polished exterior accentuated by shiny hardware. (MHF)

DOLPHIN LIKE. This pictured 1927 while hulled runabout was powered by a redundant Great War Curtiss OX-5 engine that pushed it along 40 miles per hours. Built by the Ontario Boat & Engine Works and purchased by a local business man, the Canadian Wildcat model is shown in Wallaceburg's Sydenham River upon purchase by the second owner Frank Mann who is taking his family for an outing. The company also built outboards with a unique transom well that surrounded the clamp on engine. (MHF)

MAC-CRAFT CORPORATION – 1938, Eric MacDonald established Wallaceburg's second major boat building enterprise starting on a small scale. With products under the label Mac-Craft both runabouts and utilities ranging from 15 to 21 ft. were built along with small enclosed cruisers up to 33 ft. Advertised as *"Builders of Canada's Finest Motor Boats,"* the firm built pleasure boats until 1941. Wartime forced the company to switch gears, moving to larger quarters in Sarnia to build fairmiles, small minesweepers and pontoon bridging. Two of Mac-Craft's peacetime output are shown, the 1939 double cockpit barrel back runabout (top) and the 18 ft. five passenger utility produced in 1940. (MHF)

MARINE CITY BEAUTIES. Amongst the first to organize an antique boat show was Sherman "Skip" Langell of Marine City who made arrangements with a local industry to use their Belle River property for the first 1983 show. With assistance from his wife Debbie, word circulated on both sides of the border and the inaugural event was a resounding success. Held in conjunction with Marine City's annual Maritime Days weekend event, hundreds of interested spectators flocked to the site which featured about 100 U.S. and Canadian produced pleasure craft. Growing to capacity within the space available, entrants had to be turned down to the "early registration required" event. Shown are entries in the Marine City show. (MHF)

PORT HURON ANTIQUES. When the antique boat craze hit the St. Clair River area during the 1970s, several communities organized displays of boats allowing the general public to share enjoyment. This also acted as further incentive to restore older craft that had been dormant in a barn or shed longing for tender care. Thus a new craft emerged, that of antique boat restoration. A massive hunt resulted, scouring fields, lofts, outbuildings, any place a wooden beauty might be uncovered after years of neglect. The Black River in Port Huron became a perfect venue to display boats resulting in an annual show held each September at the municipal docks. Shown are beautifully restored antique craft displayed at the 11 September 1999 Port Huron Antique and Classic Boat Show. (MHF)

ALGONAC-ANNUAL-SHOW. What is more suitable than displaying antique craft adjacent to the historic Algonac-based Chris Craft plant? And that's what folks of Michigan Chapter of the Antique & Classic Boat Club of America have done for several years. Each June invitees are asked to pull into the old Chris Craft cut, tie up their beauties and allow hundreds of attendees to marvel at the mahogany, the shiny chrome, the special added touches, all representing the rich power boat history of Algonac and area. Shown is a scene from the annual Algonac show. Arriving is Dick Eifert's 1930 Dart named *Firewood*. (MHF)

ST. CLAIR SHOW. With a beautiful setting at the St. Clair city docks on the Pine River, organizer Mark Edmonston and his crew joined in the antique boat show circuit by staging a show in this quaint community known for its salt works. Several yachts as well as runabouts from the U.S. along with Canadian visitors made the display an outstanding success. Antique vehicles on land added to the aura of the scene. Shown is Herb and Bev Anthony's 1939 Mac-Craft sedan at the 1992 St. Clair Antique & Classic Boat Show. (MHF)

WAMBO NOT RAMBO. On the Canadian side, the antique transportation interest developed into an annual display beginning in 1989. Called WAMBO (Wallaceburg Antique Motor & Boat Outing) the outstanding weekend event has evolved into Canada's foremost transportation show featuring, boats, cars, trucks, motorcycles, a fly over of antique airplanes and many other exciting and entertaining events. Entrants come from across Ontario, Michigan and Ohio with over 20,000 spectators attending the gala event held the second weekend each August. The wide array of antique boats fill the inner harbour with over 100 craft. Shown is an example of a typical entry with Richard Blackwell at the helm of his 24 ft. Greavette runabout built in 1936 and called *Canadian Club*. An annual antique boat show is also held in Sarnia each summer. (MHF)

Eight
U.S. Steel
Uncle Sam's Ships

PHILIP R. CLARKE. Sailing smoothly north of Recors Point in 1954, the Pittsburgh Steamship vessel is a veteran of the Great Lakes and still performing. Built in 1952, the vessel was lengthened in 1974 and in 1982 a self unloading device was added. A frequent sight in the St. Clair River sailing under the Great Lakes Fleet Inc., the former U.S. Steel Co. vessel is owned by the Canadian National Railways, an unusual Canada - U.S. liaison. Hopefully the vessel has many more years ahead. (Bill Abraham Collection)

NATIONAL STEEL CORPORATION. The fleet with the star on the stack is no more but was prominent on the Great Lakes for many years. One of the fleet's representatives *George M. Humphrey (2)* is upbound near Marine City in 1956. Built in Lorain, the 690 ft. straight decker was an attractive vessel even without a forward mast. A powerful ship, the *Humphrey* fought her way through the same belligerent storm that claimed the *Edmund Fitzgerald* 10 November 1975. Finished long before her time, the vessel laid up 31 December 1983 at River Rouge. Strangely on 13 August, 1986 and under her own power with a National Steel Co. alumni crew, headed for Quebec prior to a trip to Taiwan where she was towed with another fleet mate *Paul H. Carnahan* which suffered the same fate. (MHF)

CHARLES M. WHITE. Another C-4 war ship conversion adapted for Great Lakes use is shown upbound just beyond the Recors Point Detroit Edison plant north of Sombra-Marine City. Built in 1945 at Vancouver, Wash., the vessel came to Chicago from Baltimore via the Mississippi River route. Noted for power and speed the *Charles M. White* is on "full ahead" as evidenced by the bow and stern wakes. Shown in Republic Steel colours the vessel later went to Cleveland Cliffs and was dressed in their unique scheme. She sailed last in 1980 and after layup at Lorain took the tenuous tow trip to India for scrapping 1982. (Bill Abraham Collection)

SLEEPING GIANT AWAKES. After lying idle since 1981 (longer than the vessel sailed) the Interlake steamer *John Sherwin* was aroused April 11, 2006. A flag was hoisted up her mast and the tug *Minnesota* helped her to enter the Fraser Shipyard in Superior for a dry dock inspection. Built in 1958 and lengthened 96 ft. in 1973 but never outfitted with a self unloader, this surprising move by Interlake was to explore the possibility of returning the *Sherwin* to service, (much to the delight of ship fans.) (MHF)

CONVERTED CARNAHAN. Another one of the several second war vessels that came to the Great Lakes was the *Honey Hill*. A T-2 tanker built too late for action nevertheless found her niche far from Pennsylvania where she was built in 1945. Arriving in 1961, the unique bowed bulker (at 504 ft.) served with National Steel Corp. until 1985 and is seen near the Bluewater Bridge heading downbound during her first season. Another victim of a slow economy, the vessel was operated by a crew of Hanna alumni from Ecorse to Quebec City prior to her scrap trip in tow (with line mate *George M. Humphrey*) to Taiwan where the vessel was broken up in 1986-1987. (MHF)

AFTER END OF A CLYMER. Running downbound from her base at Rogers City, the *Irvin L. Clymer* is viewed upbound near Port Lambton in 1985. When built in 1917 at Lorain, the 552 ft. vessel carried a most (later) well known name *Carl D. Bradley (1)*. In 1927 to free the name for a new larger vessel (which would sink 18 November 1958 with only two survivors) the vessel was renamed *John G. Munson (1)*. In 1951 she again provided the courtesy of name giving (for another ship) and received the designation *Irvin L. Clymer* which she would carry until dismantled at Duluth in 1995. Always sailing for the Bradley (U.S.S.) fleet she was idled from 1988 to 1990 but bounced back for a final fling during which time she was photographed regularly in the St. Clair River because it was known her time was near. (MHF)

COMING ABOUT. After anchoring during a 1953 St. Clair River fog off Stokes Point (north of Sombra) the 1938-built bulker *John Hulst* is preparing to resume a downbound voyage. One of four sisters (*Governor Miller, Ralph H. Watson* and *William A. Irvin* the others) the *Hulst* did her duty until laid up in August of 1979 and scrapped in 1986, another familiar vessel in the St. Clair gone. (MHF)

PASS UNDER THE BRIDGE. The *A.E. Nettleton* of the Wilson Transit Co. enters the St. Clair River with another cargo for the lower lakes. The Wilson fleet was an integral part of the Great Lakes but regretfully passed from the scene, the white "W" seen no more. Built in Wyandotte 1908, her latter life took a strange twist being converted to a barge in 1971 but the experiment was short lived after suffering some difficulties 2 September 1972 in Lake Superior when the tow line from the tug *Olive L.Moore* parted. The vessel was laid up and in 1973 towed overseas for scrapping in Spain. (MHF)

MYRON C. TAYLOR. This early evening view of the *Myron C. Taylor* was taken 7 July 1987 as the vessel was upbound in the St. Clair River at Willow Point south of Roberts Landing. Painted in the attractive and distinctive U.S. Steel black and gray diagonal stripes, the 1929-built vessel that started out with the Bradley Transportation Co. is light and likely heading to Rogers City. This vessel was noted for her tell tale trail of smoke, a rare sight on the Great Lakes in recent years. The vessel enjoys a second life with Grand River Navigation coming over to that fleet in 2001, renamed *Calumet*. (MHF)

JOSEPH H. FRANTZ. Shown on the St. Clair River 3 July 1994 upbound just past the Recors Point power plant, this Oglebay Norton veteran *Joseph H. Frantz* is enjoying an extended life. Her small size was a strength, allowing the 1925-built vessel to operate into the late 1990s. The vessel was converted to a self unloader in 1965 making for an interesting appearance. A traditional forward cabin was in contrast to a modern aft. Surprisingly the vessel carried an "S" on her stack under Great Lakes Associates while her career was busy. However when her five year charter was terminated in 2005, the need for required work to pass inspection was too much and was towed to Port Colborne where scrapping began. (MHF)

ICE MUSH – It is the spring of 1984 and the St. Clair River is plugged with oatmeal-like ice which provides an extreme challenge for vessels caught up in its reaches. Those on shore however are entertained as the vessels struggle against the natural force. The "Mighty Mac" the well known super ice breaker *Mackinaw* (built in 1944 to keep the ice lanes open) is shown assisting Paterson's *Senator of Canada* while the *Walter A. Sterling*, a Cleveland Cliffs vessel is hoping to catch the opening. Location is north of Marine City. The *Mackinaw* was retired in 2006 and is slated to be retained as a museum ship at Cheboygan. (George Lee Collection)

ON THE RUN. The fine looking McQueen Marine tug *Amherstburg* generally works in the lower lakes but would go wherever called. Here with Capt. Cliff Morrison at the helm the tug is obviously in a hurry to answer a call, passing by Point Edward before heading into Lake Huron. The McQueen company has shared a very long history on the Great Lakes passing through more than one generation of ownership performing some of the most remarkable salvage jobs to maintain an important reputation. (Paul Michaels - Moran Collection)

GOVERNOR MILLER. A lazy summer day at Marine City's swimming area is enhanced by the upbound passage of the 593 ft. straight decker *Governor Miller* built in 1938 at Lorain. The vessel was one of four in the "Miller" class noted for tunnel passageways and a combination riveted-welded hull plates. The *Miller* along with her Miller classmates *John Hulst, Ralph H. Watson* and *William A. Irvin* were built just in time to play an important role in war, hauling iron ore in support of building vital goods that led to an Allied victory. In 1980 the vessel was retired, her final trip in the St. Clair River coming in the fall of that year eventually to make connections for a tow to Spain for scrapping. (MHF)

HENRY FORD II. No ships enjoyed a finer reputation than the Ford Motor Co. vessels, particularly the first two best known, *Benson Ford* and *Henry Ford II*. They were well maintained and noted for their two cycle single acting Sun-Doxford opposed piston diesel engines. There was no mistaking when the Ford vessels were approaching emanating their characteristic "thump, thump" sound. *Henry Ford II* was built at Lorain in 1924 known as the first large lake vessel built with diesel power. In 1974 the 592 ft. vessel was given a self unloader device at Lorain which gave her a few more years. It was a sad day indeed on 28 December 1988 when the *Henry Ford II* was laid up in the River Rouge slip, those in the know certain this was the end for the beautiful and much loved vessel. In a token move she was renamed *Samuel Mather (7)* but never sailed again under power. In December of 1994 the grand old Ford vessel was towed to Port Maitland for scrapping Between the 1967-1968 seasons the traditional stack marking with buff colouring was changed to base blue with a centre white band. Lower view shows the original scheme with a noted shiny brass steam whistle. The upper view shows the ship at buoys 1 and 2 in Lake Huron prior to entering the St. Clair River on 26 April 1987. (First photo MHF – Second photo Moran Collection)

STEINBRENNER STACK. Long a familiar stack design on the Great Lakes but the fleet known as "Kinsman" shows the funnel belonging to the venerable steamer *Frank R. Denton* shown in July of 1980. The vessel had stopped at the Shell Oil fuel dock at Froomfield. Both the horn and steam whistle are shown indicating two distinct chapters of a long career. Launched at Cleveland in 1911 for Interlake Steamship, the 580 ft. bulker also sailed for Wilson Transit until coming to Kinsman Marine. Regretfully the end came in 1982 when laid up at Buffalo. On 14 November 1984 the retired veteran was towed to Ashtabula for scrapping. (MHF)

BUCKEYE TO BARGE. A recent trend on the Great Lakes is to convert self powered vessels to barges. During 2005-2006 the *Buckeye (3)* was caught up in such a transition. (At least she will still be working!) This vessel shown 28 June 1991 downbound south of Courtright came out in 1952 as *Sparrows Point* for Bethlehem Steel. Conversion with a self unloader came in 1980. The third vessel to carry the *Buckeye* name, on 20 February 2006 the former Oglebay-Norton steamer was taken to Erie, PA to have her stern removed for the tug notch. (MHF)

STILL STEAMIN' 1906- 2006. The only Great Lakes vessel ever to operate in her 100th year, the *St. Mary's Challenger* is a most remarkable ship. Starting out as *William P. Snyder* in 1906, the 552 ft. denizen is shown approaching the St. Clair River when named *Medusa Challenger* 4 July 1986. A turning point came in 1967 when she was converted to a cement carrier, the trade engaged in ever since. Popular wherever she goes the vessel makes a number of appearances in the St. Clair River her traditional configuration a treat. (Moran Collection)

HANNAH AT DUSK. An early October 1978 evening on the placid St. Clair River near Marine City shows the *Mary Paige Hannah (2)* upbound with a barge at her bow. The attractive looking tug with an equally impressive stack, was built in 1972 as *King's Squire* for General Marine Towing and later became a fleet member with the Hannah Marine Corp. whose units are regular visitors on the St. Clair River. (George Lee Collection)

Nine
Salties in St. Clair
Far From Home

ODLAND I. Until 1960 the refined sugar trade in Canada was a viable one until the imported Cuban variety monopolized and forced the decline of the North American market. Until that time, overseas ships of pre-Seaway size were seen at smaller Canadian ports such as Wallaceburg where the Canada & Dominion Sugar Co. operation (which started in 1900) was located. Older vessels from foreign ports such as the pictured *Odland I* called at the inland port as early as the 1920s continuing in this trade until forced out by foreign competition. The *Odland I* a Norwegian vessel is shown at Wallaceburg during the 1930s. (MHF)

ROA. An early salty to the St. Clair River area *ROA* was built in 1904 as *Albert Clement* and was requisitioned by the British admiralty for service in the Great War. The vessel sailed in this capacity until 1941 and was lost without trace between Bangkok and Singapore. In better days the vessel visited the Great Lakes between the two wars and is shown at Wallaceburg in 1927. The Norwegian ship had been sent to Puerto Cortez, Honduras to pick up raw sugar which in turn was taken to Wallaceburg where she unloaded, then took on a large cargo of flax. The journey over salt and fresh water was approximately 4,000 miles. (MHF)

TALL SHIP TALL STACK?. The photographer T.L. Johnson enjoyed some camera fun by lining up the factory powerhouse stack in line with the ship's funnel. The Norwegian salty *Brush* (251 ft.) had sailed directly to Wallaceburg from overseas to pick up a load of freshly refined sugar at the Canada & Dominion Sugar Co. in Wallaceburg. The vessel had lots of open water on the long journey but the master must have been experiencing trauma when heading inland through the many twists and turns of the narrow Chenal Ecarte and Sydenham Rivers. The ship, built in 1939 nevertheless experienced little difficulty and actually returned to the inland port the next year. (MHF)

SAMARU. The last salt water vessel known to travel inland at the Chenal Ecarte (but not very far) was the 1957-built German vessel *Pluto* which was renamed *Samaru* by the time she was refitted in temporary layup near Ecarte Marina at Port Lambton. In the summer of 1980 the vessel had been to Collingwood for some work and eventually departed Port Lambton 29 November 1981 when purchased by Harry Gamble Marine of Port Dover after which the vessel went to the Caribbean for further work. Scene shows *Samaru* arriving at Port Lambton in the summer of 1980. (MHF)

LITTLE CALM ON THE MONTCALM – Since the vessel is stuck, the captain and crew of this Russian ship *Montcalm* are likely impatient and agitated. On 28 November 1963 the 245 ft. vessel was downbound in Lake Huron heading for Sarnia to take on cargo. Near the Huron lightship a shoal came up suddenly and grabbed the vessel. McQueen Marine was called to free the vessel with the tug's line shown pulling at the bow. (Al Jackson Collection)

FRENCH LINE VISITOR. The attractive French visitor *Uranus* is moored along side the Sarnia government wharf 29 May 1963. The vessel was built in 1963 and was on her very first visit through the Seaway system. She stopped at Sarnia to take on locally produced cargo before continuing her trip up the Lakes to take on more North American goods. (Al Jackson Collection)

VIBYHOLM. This Swedish vessel first passed through the Seaway system in 1960. Built in 1951 at 431 ft., her pictured Sarnia visit came 17 June 1963 where the "light" coloured vessel took on cargo. *Vibyholm* was noted for her most attractive appearance and drew a number of visitors to the Sarnia waterfront in admiration. (Al Jackson Collection)

ISRAELIAN VISITOR. The prominent high bow flare designed to fight off oft vicious ocean waves, caught the eyes of Sarnia harbour visitors in 1964. Shown during a 14 August visit that year is *Etrog* registered in Israel. This ship was brand new, launched the same year she came to the Great Lakes and included Sarnia as a port of call during her visit. Many came to the waterfront to view the new vessel. (Al Jackson Collection)

TRANSAMERICA. With such an appropriate name it is little wonder this attractively appointed salt water vessel was well received in North America. Representing the Poseiden Line this 1948-built salt water ship made a number of visits to the St. Clair River area. At 388 ft. in length she touched in at Sarnia on the pictured arrival 14 May 1963 but had visited the port first in 1960 so she knew her way to the local government wharf where she is moored. (Al Jackson Collection)

TRAMP STEAMER? - Perhaps not classed as such but the *Prinses Irene* from Rotterdam was part of the Oranje Line's combining cargo and passengers on their vessels coming to North America. The experiment proved popular and *Prinses Irene* became known in this unique post war trade. The vessel is in Sarnia 29 July 1963. While cargo is being taken aboard, passengers were allowed to depart and stretch their legs. *Prinses Irene* was built in 1959 and the first vessel built specifically for this type of North American trade. Capacity was 110 passengers all in one class. (Al Jackson Collection)

BEACHED AND BLACKENED. On 6 October 1966, the 392 ft. German vessel *Emsstein* collided with the Greek ship *Olympic Pearl* in the St. Clair River opposite the Lambton Generating plant south of Courtright. The *Emsstein* was holed due to the collision and eventually settled like a beached whale her starboard flank exposed to the many who came to view the spectacle. An electrical fire caused considerable damage to the hull's interior. McQueen Marine of Amherstburg was contracted to right and repair the vessel. (George Lee Collection)

Ten
Ferrying Frequently
Back & Forth

HIAWATHA. This rather tiny vessel built in 1874 served on various excursion routes until called upon to shuttle passengers between Sarnia and Port Huron. Once the Huron and Erie rail line was extended north from Wallaceburg to Sarnia (officially opened 3 September 1886) relying on excursion boats for travel declined. The *Hiawatha* was affected and shortly thereafter was employed on the cross river ferry route. Later replaced by more modern vessels, *Hiawatha* went north in 1925 to Little Current ending her days beached on Red Mill Island. (MHF)

HERE COME THE CITY FOLK! - The *Theodore Roosevelt, Put-In-Bay* and occasionally the White Star Steamers would run special excursions to Walpole Island allowing city folk to attend the annual Indian Fair. This scene in the late 1920s shows one such occasion as the Canadian Customs officers await to check through the U.S. visitors who would return with Indian crafts and souvenirs a few hours later (along with yawns and yearning for some rest.) The historic heritage building on land (centre) remains as a reminder of another era. (MHF)

MARY C.. Ferry service between Courtright and St. Clair lasted nearly 100 years, terminating in November 1964. Cross river service began in the mid 1860s with a rowboat owned by Joseph Gallineau. Various launches and barges followed with service improving. The pictured *Mary C.* and another unit *Marilyn M.* were operated by Frank Currier, the latter continuing until 1956 when a new large nine auto self powered vessel was put into service. The tiny *Mary C.* offered weather protection with full around wrapping complete with small round peep holes for the captain. (MHF)

TIGER BRAND. When few had autos but pleasure beckoned (and Tashmoo Park at Sans Souci was the destination) Fuller's Ferry Service filled the bill. Seven round trips a day connected Algonac on the mainland to Tashmoo Park on Harsen's Island. This 1920s service on the *Tiger* also meant convenient connections with the passenger steamers *Tashmoo, Wauketa* and *City of Toledo*. (MHF)

HERE SHE COMES, MISS AMERICA! This ferry launch exuded "boat beauty" with her gleaming white hull and classic styling. Owned by the Whitely Ferry Line that operated between Sombra and Marine City, the former *Catherine M.* offered connecting service with trains on both sides of the river. In fact, if owner Tom Whitely had a passenger wanting to catch the Pere Marquette train at Sombra station, he would signal five blasts on his horn hoping to catch the attention of the train engineer who would generally wait. In the background downbound is the gunboat *U.S.S. Dubuque*. (Gene Buel Collection)

MASCOT. Cross river ferry service from Port Lambton to Roberts Landing dates back to 1880 when a row boat was used to shuttle passengers. Cost was .05 cents. Transportation methods advanced when a launch and barge were used, George Roberts of Detroit one of the first to utilize this means. Webster Dawson took over the service in 1919 with the photo showing his launch *Mascot* just completing the "swing around" of the barge. Two generations of the Dawson family operated the service until 1958 when the business was sold. (Marguerite Myers Collection)

KEEP THE LINE! - Before self-propelled ferries, launches and barges provided service between Walpole Island and Algonac. The captain ran the launch and a deckhand stood watch on the barge that would carry as many as four automobiles. As long as the weather was clear and the wind was down, things went well, but rue the days when heavy winds and white caps challenged the ferry operator to swing the barge around at just the right angle. Two piece service of this nature lasted through the early days of the second war. Shown is the launch *Rita* departing Walpole Island about 1939. (MHF)

THE LAST WALPOLE WOODIE. Used first on the mainland to Harsen's Island run beginning in 1932, the wooden self propelled ferry *WIT* provided dependable service until Art Champion built a steel ferry for the route in 1939. Registered in Canada under the name *Ariel D.* operated by Capt. Morgan Dalgety, the six car capacity hull ran the Walpole-Algonac route until 1946 when the first steel ferry *Lowell D.* arrived. The *Ariel D.* was later abandoned in the east passage of the Chenal Ecarte in the early 1950s. (MHF)

LOWELL D. A new era arrived in 1946 when the diesel ferry *Lowell D.* built in Erieau by Goodison Industries arrived for service on the Walpole Island to Algonac ferry run. Much more powerful than any previous ferries, several additional runs per day could be completed. As well the steel hull could withstand ice that would otherwise halt the service. Many Walpole Island residents were employed in Algonac at the Chris Craft plant and depended on prompt and regular service to the United States. When the new *Walpole Islander* arrived in 1986, the *Lowell D.* was used only occasionally and eventually was sold and used at Colchester as a dive ship. (MHF)

QUEEN MARY. Not of the Cunard liner family, this 65 ft. wooden gasoline ferry was the last to operate on the Courtright to St. Clair ferry run. Capt. Sherwood Anderson decided to update and purchased the *Queen Mary* which had operated between Redbank, New Jersey to Philadelphia. Capt. Sherwood Anderson and Ray Ingles began a 21 day odyssey that required them to cut down the pilot house in the Erie Canal to go under bridges, spend time in the open Atlantic Ocean, burn out a waterpump, run into a strong tide that opened up caulking seams, partially sink the hull to go under a bridge and lose power in Lake Erie. With other minor mishaps they made it to the St. Clair River in June of 1956. The next year Tate Clarke and Ron Purdy took over and refitted the *Courtright* shown at Purdy Fisheries, Point Edward in 1957. In 1959 Lowell Dalgety purchased the ferry, operating the service until 1964 when Ted and Wm. Glass took over. However a failed hull inspection terminated the service at the end of the 1964 season. (Ray Ingles Collection)

NOWHERE TO GO – It is March 1975 and a brisk north wind has jammed the St. Clair River chock full of heavy lake ice. Normally ferry service could operate unimpeded in March but not this time. The Port Lambton ferry *Ontamich* is jammed and has to await the St. Clair clearing. Commuters were forced to go the long way around via the Bluewater Bridge as the other two ferry services at Walpole Island and Sombra were also locked in by ice. The *Ontamich*, built originally for the Harsen's Island run, worked Port Lambton-Roberts Landing until the service terminated in 1985, then reverted to the Sombra-Marine City route. (MHF)

HIGH AND DRY. Rather then head downriver to dry dock in the Windsor area, ferry owner Capt. Lowell Dalgety decided to use a new approach for the required Dept. of Transport five year hull inspection. A large crane from Sarnia was hired to lift the ferry *Daldean* from the water and gently place the 1951-built steel hull on land just a few yards from her landing dock. The experiment proved successful and once the inspection was completed, the reverse process was carried out. In the meantime, the *Ontamich* (built in 1939 as *Harsens Island*) continued the service from Sombra to Marine City. (MHF)

MOVIE STAR. With Master Dale Dean at the helm, the *Walpole Islander* wandered somewhat from her usual run to Algonac to star in a film production. During August of 1996 Spy Films of Toronto shot a Pontiac Sunfire tv commercial in Wallaceburg. Plot saw the new car late catching a ferry just as a bridge (Lord Selkirk over the Sydenham River) was lifted. View shows the car (attached to a crane) being lowered onto the ferry deck as part of the sequence. The commercial was aired in the fall of 1996 with the ferry in a supporting role. (MHF)

Eleven
Preservation
Museum Quality

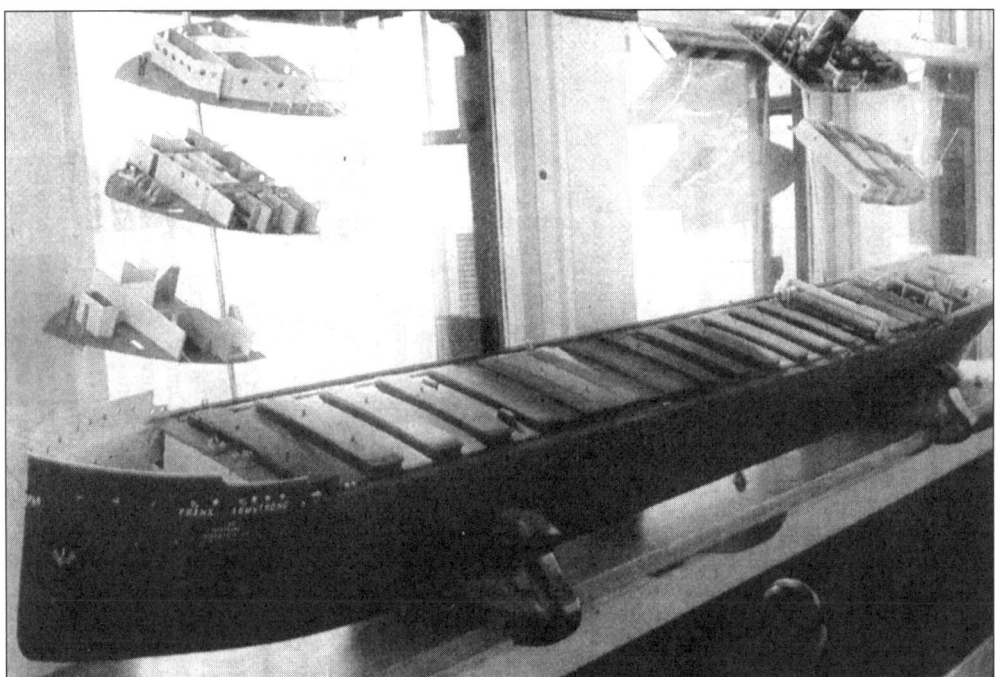

ALGONAC/CLAY TOWNSHIP HISTORICAL SOCIETY COMMUNITY MUSEUM
(1240 St. Clair River Dr., Algonac, MI. 48001 (810)-794-9015 www.algonac-clay. history.org)

The museum features extensive displays relating to local boat building particularly Chris Craft Corporation at one time the world's largest producers of pleasure craft. Also, items in connection with Gar Wood, local resident who held world supremacy in unlimited powerboat racing, are featured. Other displays include a part by part applied freighter model, other ship models and photos and items related to the Great Lakes. Shown is a model of the Interlake vessel *Frank Armstrong*, a maritime class bulk carrier built in 1943. The vessel, 620 ft. in length operated until 1981. The model was built by Alan Wilson, a deck watchman aboard the vessel in 1945.

PRIDE & HERITAGE MUSEUM - MARINE CITY
(405 S. Main St., Marine City, MI. 48039, (810)-765-5446)

Once known as Newport, honoured is Marine City's rich marine heritage where hundreds of ships were built. A number of interesting display artifacts connected to marine history are displayed including ship models; a wide array of photos, ship building tools as well as items related to powerboat racing. Highlight is an extensive ship diorama depicting Marine City's prominent connection to shipping on the St. Clair River. The building, originally Newport Academy (established in 1845) became the Pride & Heritage Museum in 1983. Also of interest on the waterfront is the former Peche Island Lighthouse, built in 1908 and moved to Marine City in 1982 following decommissioning. Shown are visitors in the Marine Display area.

MARYSVILLE HISTORICAL MUSEUM
(887 E.Huron Blvd., Marysville, MI. 48040 (810)-364-6613)

Marine displays include 12 models of ships that sailed the Great Lakes and St. Clair River. Each model has a description of when the ship was put into use and when it sunk or was taken out of service. A beautiful model of the 1944-built ice breaker *Mackinaw* is one of the highlights along with various artifacts and photos related to the shipping industry and the St. Clair River area. South of Marysville is located the city of St. Clair Historical Museum which features a number of displays related to the St. Clair River and Great Lakes areas. Shown is the *Mackinaw* model representing the famed icebreaker that passed upbound in the St. Clair River during 2006 prior to retirement.

PORT HURON MUSEUM CARNEGIE CENTRE
(1115 Sixth St., Port Huron, MI. 48060 (810)-982-0891 www.phmuseum.org)

Established in 1967 in the former Port Huron Library, the museum offers the most extensive marine display in the St. Clair River area. The Lee Cooper Marine Gallery features models, whistles, paintings, photos and a wide array of artifacts related to Great Lakes history including the St. Clair River. Hands-on items are available. The Frank Crevier pilot house provides a realistic early 20th century view from the bridge of a ship entering Lake Huron. On the grounds, a rudder from the schooner *William H. Shupe* is displayed as well as anchors from the *John Martin* and *Fontana*. The lightship *Huron*, coast guard vessel *Bramble*, along with the *Fort Gratiot Lighhouse* are also included as part of the museum's living history displays.

LAMBTON HERITAGE MUSEUM
(Highway 21, 8 km. South of Grand Bend, ON. (519)-243-2600   www.lclmg.org)

The Lambton County Museum includes a number of items related to the Great Lakes. Featured is a tribute case to Northwest Transportation Co., an index of Great Lakes freighters from the Garnet Peachey Collection. A number of items pay tribute to the Northern Navigation Division of Canada Steamship Lines such as the *Hamonic* wheelhouse plaque, Capt. Horace Beaton's masters cap, a post card set, menu and song book from the *Hamonic* and a wooden gift ship pin. A photo portrait of Henry Beattie looks down on a model of *Old Bessie* (more properly known as *United Empire*) in 1884. This was installed as a tribute to the founder of Canada's first navigation firm operating on the upper Great Lakes. The museum also holds a wide collection of views photographed by renowned Great Lakes photographer Louis Pesha.

MOORE MUSEUM
(94 Moore Line, Mooretown, On (519) 867-2020 www.lambtononline.com.moore-museum)

Moore Museum's Great Lakes collection includes equipment (including compasses, lights, life rings and life jackets) photographs of ships, models of freighters and passenger ships, ship's china, a hand-painted window from the salon of the *Huronic* and a model and life ring from the *Edmund Fitzgerald*. On the grounds is the 1890 rear range light from Corunna. Shown are models of the Northern Navigation passenger steamers *Hamonic* and *Noronic*, photos of the ships, a china plate and in the background a series of sketches showing vessels of the Soo River Line.

SOMBRA MUSEUM
(3470 St. Clair Parkway: Sombra, ON. (519)892-3982)

An extensive marine room displays ships models of *Daldean, Wm. A. Reiss, Amoco Indiana* and other non Great Lakes models. Various items of marine electronic equipment are displayed as well as brass items, a life ring from the ill-fated *Carl D. Bradley*, a life preserver from the ferry *WIT*, oars from the *A.E. Nettleton* and the ship's wheel from the carferry *Daldean* are featured. An extensive resource file is available for research including information about local captains. Alleged items from La Salle's *Griffon* are displayed as well as components from Al Capone's yacht *Compass Rose*. Reminders of rum running days along the St. Clair River are remembered along with a wide display of crockery and ship making tools. A number of Northern Navigation items are highlighted. Photos depict the Marine Room display including the *Daldean's* wheel, ship models and an array of miscellaneous Great Lakes items. A Canada Steamship Lines fleet flag is displayed and a painting of the schooner *Hattie Hutt*.

WALLACEBURG & DISTRICT MUSEUM
(505 King St. Wallaceburg, ON. (519) 627-8962   www.kent.net/wallaceburg-museum)

Included within the museum is an extensive marine display area. A pilot house interior, circa 1900 has been re-created with appropriate items including a chadburn from the Canada Steamship canaller *City of Toronto* which called to the port of Wallaceburg regularly. A ship builders model of the steamer *D. A. Gordon* built in Scotland is shown along with other models. A hull portion and funnel from the locally built steamer *Annette Fraser*, along with shipbuilding tools feature a special display. Home to three powerboat builders, models and items relating to the *Ontario Boat & Engine Works*, *Mac*-Craft *Corporation* and *Van-Craft* are displayed. Various other marine items as related to Wallaceburg- known as Canada's Inland Deep Water Port are displayed.

HURON LIGHTSHIP and U.S.COAST GUARD VESSEL BRAMBLE
(located on shoreline at Pine Grove Park, Port Huron, MI.)

What better way to preserve history than to have a living example! When lightship *No.103* was decommissioned 25 August 1970, members of Lake Huron Lore Marine Society and others interested rallied to see that the small ship beacon was preserved. Built in 1920 at Morris Heights, N.Y., the lightship was used at various Great Lakes sites until 1934 when it was assigned to lower Lake Huron guiding shipping in and out of the St. Clair River. After volunteer refurbishing the, lightship was permanently moored at Pine Grove Park. A more recent companion for the display is the retired U.S. Coast Guard vessel *Bramble* (WLB-392) decommissioned in 2003 which will be opened for public tours. Both vessels are displays under the Port Huron Museum of Arts and History.

LAKE HURON LORE MARINE SOCIETY
(headquarters at Port Huron Museum of Arts and History)

One of the most active marine study groups on the Great Lakes is the Lake Huron Lore Marine Society. Often partnering with the Detroit Marine Historical Society, regular entertainment programs are offered along with study and preservation of marine history particularly the St. Clair River. An example was the program, "Old Charts and Steam Whistles" which attracted an enthusiastic gathering. Incorporated in the State of Michigan October 21, 1963, Lake Huron distributes a newsletter "The Lightship" and gatherings are open to the public. For information: www.lakehuronlore.com

BLOW IT AGAIN SAM! - Preservation of Great Lakes ship sounds in the form of whistle blows created a new interest in marine history. During the 1970s, such gatherings "gained steam" with meets held at Marine City, St. Clair and a gala gathering at the Marysville Edison power plant where actual steam was used adding authenticity to both the sound and cosmetic appeal. The gatherings held annually required a diligent effort from the pipe wrench crew but they were aficionados themselves. Once a whistle was hooked up, the crew stepped back and soaked up the sounds like everyone else. Huge brass whistles from many vessels were heard, but the favourites were the beautiful and nostalgic reverberations from the famed passenger steamers *Tashmoo* and *South American*. The sounds evoked old memories for those present who had been fortunate enough to grace the decks of these once proud ships of the Great Lakes.

Twelve
Canadian Content
Red Maple Leafs

C.S.L. NIPIGON BAY. With a freshly painted Canada Steamship Lines stack, yet still in Esso colours, the newly named *Nipigon Bay* is downbound at Port Lambton in 1954 during transition. Built as *Imperial Leduc* at Collingwood, the massive 620 ft. tanker was no longer needed since a pipeline from the west was completed to Sarnia. C.S.L. purchased the tanker, converted it to a bulk carrier and she worked until 2 December 1982 when laid up at Montreal with scrapping coming during 1989 in Turkey. (MHF)

GET ME LOOSE! – Stuck in the mud is costly for the owners and downright frustrating (needless to say embarrassing for the captain.) The venerable Canada Steamship Lines bulker *Gleneagles* went slightly off course in the St. Clair River north of Roberts Landing in July of 1957 near light 37. After some valiant tugging by the Great Lakes rigs *Maryland* and *Superior*, *Gleneagles* was eventually freed after drawing much attention. Launched at Midland 26 August 1925 she worked for C.S.L. until 1978 and remaining years came under the name *Silverdale* for Dale Transport with final layup at Windsor coming 23 November 1983 and scrapping two years later. (George Lee Collection)

KINGDOC AT REST – Secure at the Sarnia government wharf 24 November 1986, Paterson's *Kingdoc (2)* was built by Davie Shipbuilding at Lauzon and launched August 1963. Built also for coastal duties, the vessel left the Lakes two years after this Sarnia visit and worked in various foreign waters. With her new owners Polaris Navigation, the vessel went overseas and in 1990 was sold again and renamed *Lucky Star*, and in 1995 was *Caroline F*. It is quite amazing how an innocent looking vessel in the small port of Sarnia would sail the world. (MHF)

IMPERIAL LONDON. Another Esso beauty built at Collingwood, the 258 ft. tanker was launched in 1948, installed with a Skinner unaflow *1200* hp. steam engine. The tanker was lengthened twice with final configuration of 331 ft. as shown in Sarnia during 1971. Six years later the tanker was finished for Imperial Oil and sold to Honduran interests but she is remembered for her attachment with Sarnia and the St. Clair River area. (MHF)

B.A. ALL THE WAY! - Issuing a salute while passing downbound at Marine City, the *Britamolene*, a British American Oil Co. tanker is on her way. Built in England and launched 19 May 1931, the vessel crossed the wide Atlantic to fulfill duties on the Great Lakes. This 1947 scene shows the 258 ft. vessel, which was later purchased by Hall Corporation in 1959 and renamed *Wave Transport*. Later the tanker ended up in South America where she operated until 1982, her interesting career spanning three continents. (MHF)

BURNED OUT AND UNWANTED. Once a proud and speedy "new breed" package freighter for Canada Steamship, the 461 ft. vessel was launched at Collingwood 15 January 1958. She worked effectively for several years speeding through the St. Clair River occasionally stopping at Sarnia. By the 1980s work was less and in 1984 was sold for scrap With a brief reprieve, the stern was notched for a push barge, but this did not work out and she was laid up at the Point Edward freight shed suffering neglect and a vandalized fire. Shown languishing there the tug *Tusker* is at her bow 25 October, 1987 ready to depart for eventual scrapping in Brazil during 1988. (Dick Wicklund Collection)

NEW LEASE ON LIFE. On her first call to Sarnia 12 December 2005 in her sparkling new blue livery, *Voyageur Independent* is most impressive. As *Kinsman Independent (3)* the 642 ft. vessel established the distinction of being the last U.S. straight decker. After layup in December of 2002 at Hamilton, her future was grim. However, McKeil Marine picked her up, in turn, owned by Wayne Elliott, who put the vessel back into operation for a new company Voyageur Marine Transport Ltd. of Ridgeville, Ontario. This was a most surprising turn of events for the 1952-built vessel which was launched as *Charles L. Hutchinson (3)* for Pioneer Steamship. She was *Ernest R. Breech* from 1962 to 1988. (Blake Mann Photo)

TRANSITION. With cosmetic change underway for transformation from U.S. Steel to Lower Lakes Towing, the "old colours" stack is intact as is the name *G.A. Sloan Co. No. 1* on the starboard lifeboat. But the painters have been busy as the new name *Mississagi* has been identified on the aft section of the 1943-built vessel that briefly carried the name *Hill Annex* before being named *George A. Sloan*, the designation carried for 58 years. Transition time in the Sarnia-Point Edward area during the spring of 2001 drew interest from across the Great Lakes area. (MHF)

STADACONA (3). If beauty determined longevity, this handsome C.S.L. self unloader would sail forever. However, the cruelty of time was her eventual downfall. The vessel was launched at Port Arthur in 1952 as the straight decker *Thunder Bay*. The 646 ft. vessel took on her pictured name in 1969. Shown at her best under the Bluewater Bridge 14 June 1987, the Canada Steamship vessel was laid up in Windsor 31 July 1990, another victim of time. The Great Lakes was poorer when STADACONA was behind the tow line heading for scrapping in China during 1993. (Moran Collection)

NANCY A. LEE. Typical of small local tugs around the Great Lakes and adjoining rivers, the Lee Marine tug *Nancy A. Lee* is shown on the St. Clair River. She was built by Russel Brothers at Owen Sound in 1939. The small 40 ft. tug was initially used as a fishing vessel. With Lee Marine she carries out light towing duties and transfers sailors to and from ships. For several years the popular tug has carried members of Lake Huron Lore's *Apple Dumpling Gang* on an annual fall colour cruise to Wallaceburg. (George Lee Collection)

BOLAND TO SAGINAW. Another sign of transition in Sarnia harbour was evidenced in November of 1999 when the former *John J. Boland (3)* built in 1953, was taking on a new appearance as *Saginaw* for Lower Lakes Towing Co. A number of ships thought to be finished were purchased by this Port Dover-based company, refitted and put back into service. A number of such transfers took place beginning in 1995 when the former *J. Burton Ayers* became *Cuyahoga* with the most recent in 2003 with the former *Elton Hoyt 2nd* becoming *Michipicoten (2)*. (MHF)

IMPERIAL SARNIA. With her flags fluttering, the brand new *Imperial Sarnia* enters the St. Clair River under the Blue Water Bridge in 1948 fresh from her construction in Collingwood. The vessel, closely attached over the years to her namesake port, did sail for a spell in South America and also in the far north but was most comfortable in the St. Clair River. Sailing days ended in the late fall of 1986, when, under her own power, Capt. Nate Smith took her to Hamilton where she became a fuel storage barge named *Provmar Terminal II.* (John Philbin Collection)

JUDITH'S STACK. While resting during refuelling at Shell's Froomfield dock in July of 1979 the Soo River shamrock of the *Judith M. Pierson* cools briefly. Built in 1917 as *William A. Amberg*, her senior years are evident with the double barrel whistle chambers representing a sign of antiquity. But those sweet sounds that would emanate from the whistles, acted as music to the ears for many due to rarity by the 1970s. The vessel came into Canadian ownership in 1975 for a few extra years of operation with Soo River Co. "Finished with engines" came in 1982, another chapter closed. (MHF)

BON VOYAGE – As the *Hamonic* sails away into the distance, so ends this journey on the St. Clair River. Whether it is the placid calm of an early summer sunrise morning or the agitated white caps of a wind strewn afternoon, the St. Clair retains its glory. It is a sanctuary for the ships that ply its water but at the same time a panorama of sights and sounds for those looking towards from the shorelines. Sail on St. Clair and may your flowing beauty continue to be a representative of nature's best. (MHF)